5 Ingredients

Instant Pot

Cookbook for Beginners

2000+ Days of Instant Pot Recipes for Beginners, No Stress, Just 5 Ingredients or Even Less for A Healthy Meal, No Matter the Occasion, You'll be The Most Dazzling Chef!

Instant Pot

Marion W. Laird

CONTENTS

INTRODUCTION

The Instant Pot has gained a reputation as one of the most versatile and convenient kitchen appliances available today, revolutionizing home cooking and meal preparation. It was originally developed by Robert Wang and his Canadian-based team in 2010, with the intention of simplifying complex cooking tasks by combining multiple appliances into one. The result was an electric pressure cooker with capabilities that extended well beyond pressure cooking alone, including slow cooking, rice cooking, steaming, yogurt making, and even warming functions. This multi-functionality quickly won over home chefs and busy families alike, making it a must-have in modern kitchens.

The device became especially popular due to its ability to consistently produce well-cooked, flavorful dishes without requiring constant monitoring or adjustments. Users can simply set their desired cooking time and function, and the Instant Pot takes care of the rest, freeing up time and energy for other tasks. Its user-friendly design, compact structure, and ability to cook dishes faster than conventional methods make it a highly valuable tool, especially in households where time-saving without sacrificing quality is a top priority. Over time, new models with enhanced features like Wi-Fi connectivity and customizable settings have made it even more accessible and popular, turning it into a culinary staple for millions worldwide.

The Instant Pot's widespread popularity reflects not only the quality of its design but also its adaptability to a range of cooking styles, diets, and culinary traditions. Whether you're cooking stews, soups, meats, grains, or desserts, the Instant Pot's precision and flexibility cater to a wide array of needs. It allows home cooks to experiment with recipes that would traditionally take hours and simplifies meal preparation for anyone, from beginners to experienced chefs.

Advantages of the Instant Pot

The Instant Pot's appeal lies in the extensive advantages it offers. Below, we explore these benefits in greater depth:

Time Efficiency: Traditional cooking methods can take hours to prepare meals, especially when it comes to foods like stews, roasts, and legumes. The Instant Pot reduces cooking times dramatically by using high-pressure steam to cook foods quickly, while retaining their moisture and flavor. For instance, beans that would typically take over an hour on the stovetop can be ready in 20 minutes in an Instant Pot, while tough cuts of meat become tender in half the usual time. This time-saving aspect makes the Instant Pot invaluable for busy individuals or families who still want to enjoy homemade meals without sacrificing hours in the kitchen.

Space-Saving and Multi-Functional: The Instant Pot is a multi-cooker, meaning it combines the functions of several kitchen appliances into one. It can serve as a pressure cooker, slow cooker, rice cooker, steamer, yogurt maker, and even a sauté pan. By consolidating these functionalities, the Instant Pot helps save valuable counter and storage space, which is particularly beneficial for those with smaller kitchens. There's no need to invest in or store multiple separate appliances, as the Instant Pot handles a variety of cooking tasks, making it a single appliance solution for a wide range of recipes and techniques.

Energy Efficiency: The Instant Pot's insulated design and quicker cooking process allow it to use less energy compared to conventional ovens and stovetops. This makes it not only time-efficient but also energy-efficient, helping users reduce electricity usage, which is both economical and environmentally friendly. The device heats up quickly, maintains temperature well, and cooks in a sealed environment, all of which contribute to its energy savings over longer cooking methods.

Enhanced Nutritional Retention: The Instant Pot's quick cooking at high pressure helps foods retain their nutrients more effectively compared to traditional cooking methods, which often expose foods to heat for extended periods. Nutritional studies have shown that pressure-cooked vegetables and meats retain more vitamins and minerals compared to boiling or prolonged simmering. For health-conscious individuals or families, this means meals prepared in the Instant Pot can offer enhanced nutritional value, preserving delicate nutrients in fruits, vegetables, and meats.

Even Cooking with Flavor Enhancement: The sealed environment of the Instant Pot prevents moisture from escaping, allowing flavors to concentrate and ingredients to cook evenly. This feature is particularly valuable for meats, stews, and soups, which benefit from enhanced flavors and tender textures. Additionally, since the Instant Pot cooks in a pressurized environment, it encourages the blending of flavors, making dishes richer and more flavorful. This advantage has made it a preferred method for preparing complex, layered dishes that would otherwise require long cooking times and careful monitoring.

How the Instant Pot Operates

The Instant Pot utilizes advanced pressure cooking technology to revolutionize the way we prepare meals. At its core, the operation of the Instant Pot is centered around its ability to create a sealed environment where steam can build up, resulting in high pressure and temperature.

This is achieved through a combination of a robust heating element and a meticulously designed inner pot that conducts heat efficiently.

When you start cooking with the Instant Pot, you first add your ingredients and a specified amount of liquid—water, broth, or another cooking medium—into the inner pot. Once the lid is securely locked in place, the heating element activates and begins to heat the contents. As the liquid reaches its boiling point, steam is generated. In a traditional pot, this steam would escape into the atmosphere, but the Instant Pot keeps it contained, allowing the pressure to build.

The unique design of the Instant Pot includes a pressure regulator that automatically adjusts the pressure inside the pot, ensuring it remains stable throughout the cooking process. As pressure increases, the boiling point of the liquid rises above 100 degrees Celsius (212 degrees Fahrenheit), allowing food to cook faster than in normal atmospheric conditions. For example, tough cuts of meat, which typically require hours of slow cooking, can become fork-tender in a fraction of the time.

Moreover, the Instant Pot is equipped with a microprocessor that meticulously monitors and controls cooking parameters, including temperature and pressure. This high-tech feature allows for precision cooking, ensuring that foods are cooked evenly and thoroughly without the risk of burning or drying out. The appliance also offers various cooking modes, such as "Pressure Cook," "Slow Cook," "Steam," and "Saute," each tailored to different types of dishes and cooking techniques.

One of the standout features of the Instant Pot is its dual pressure settings—high and low—which allows users to select the appropriate level based on the type of food being cooked. For instance, high pressure is ideal for cooking grains, beans, and meats, while low pressure can be used for more delicate foods like fish or vegetables, helping to preserve their texture and nutritional value.

After the cooking cycle is complete, the Instant Pot provides two options for releasing pressure: natural release and quick release. Natural release allows the pressure to drop on its own, which can take anywhere from 10 to 30 minutes, depending on the amount of food and liquid inside. This method is best for dishes that benefit from resting, such as stews or roasts. Conversely, quick release involves manually opening the steam valve, which rapidly expels steam. This method is perfect for quick-cooking items like vegetables or rice that need to be served immediately.

In summary, the Instant Pot's operation is a harmonious blend of traditional cooking techniques and modern technology, allowing for a diverse range of cooking methods that make meal preparation faster and more efficient. By harnessing the power of steam and pressure, it transforms cooking into a straightforward, user-friendly experience, making it an indispensable tool in any kitchen.

Usage Tips for the Instant Pot

Making the most out of an Instant Pot requires an understanding of some key tips and techniques:

Understand Pressure Release Types: Each release method has its ideal application. For foods like vegetables or delicate cuts of meat, a quick release is preferable, as it prevents overcooking. For tougher meats, soups, and stews, the natural release method is ideal, allowing the steam to dissipate gradually, which helps retain moisture and tenderness.

Use the Sauté Function: Unlike traditional pressure cookers, the Instant Pot offers a sauté function, allowing you to brown meats or cook down aromatics directly in the pot before adding liquids. This adds depth and complexity to flavors, as you can caramelize onions or sear meats before pressure cooking. Additionally, the sauté function can be used post-cooking to reduce or thicken sauces, adding versatility to the appliance.

Avoid Overfilling: It's crucial to follow the fill line on the inner pot, especially when cooking foods that expand (like rice, beans, or pasta). Overfilling the pot can cause pressure to build up too quickly, which may impact cooking performance or cause food to spurt out of the steam valve. As a general rule, don't fill the pot more than two-thirds full for most foods, and no more than halfway for items that expand.

Layer Ingredients for Even Cooking: When cooking dishes with multiple ingredients, consider the density and cooking times of each component. Heavier items like root vegetables or meats should go at the bottom, closer to the heat source, while lighter ingredients like leafy greens should be added on top. This layering ensures that all ingredients cook evenly and enhances the flavors.

Experiment with Pre-Set Programs: The Instant Pot comes with various pre-set functions tailored to different cooking tasks, like "Porridge," "Soup," or "Stew." These programs are optimized to control pressure and temperature for specific types of food, making it easy to cook certain dishes without much guesswork. Experimenting with these settings can help simplify meal prep, ensuring that each dish is cooked to perfection.

Utilize the Pot-in-Pot (PIP) Method: The Pot-in-Pot method allows you to cook multiple components at once without mixing flavors. By placing a smaller heat-safe dish on a trivet within the Instant Pot, you can cook side dishes or desserts alongside the main meal. This method is ideal for preparing foods that require different seasonings or textures, such as rice with curry or meat with a vegetable side.

Cleaning and Maintenance of the Instant Pot

Proper cleaning and maintenance are essential to prolonging the lifespan of your Instant Pot and keeping it in excellent condition.

Remove and Clean the Sealing Ring: The silicone sealing ring in the lid traps odors and flavors easily. It's a good idea to remove it after each use and clean it thoroughly. For persistent odors, soak the ring in a solution of vinegar and water. The ring is also dishwasher-safe, but hand washing can help prevent it from wearing out prematurely.

Clean the Inner Pot and Accessories: The stainless steel inner pot is durable and dishwasher-safe, but hand-washing it with a non-abrasive sponge will maintain its shine longer. Avoid metal or rough sponges, which can scratch the surface, and ensure that all accessories—such as the trivet, steam rack, and utensils—are cleaned thoroughly to prevent buildup.

Wipe Down the Lid and Exterior: To prevent food residue or grime from building up, wipe down the lid and exterior of the Instant Pot with a damp cloth after each use. Pay particular attention to the steam release valve, anti-block shield, and float valve, as these areas are more likely to become clogged with food particles.

Descale the Inner Pot When Needed: If you live in an area with hard water, mineral deposits can accumulate on the inner pot over time. Descaling it with a mixture of vinegar and water heated on the "Sauté" function helps to remove this buildup, ensuring your pot remains clean and functional.

Inspect the Sealing Components Regularly: Every few months, inspect the sealing ring, float valve, and anti-block shield for any signs of wear or damage. Replacing the sealing ring every 12-18 months is recommended, as the silicone can degrade with regular use, affecting the pot's ability to seal properly.

Store Properly to Prevent Odors: When storing your Instant Pot, leave the lid slightly ajar to allow airflow, which helps prevent odors from becoming trapped. Storing the pot in a dry, cool area away from temperature extremes will help maintain its electrical components and extend its longevity.

Breakfast Recipes

Breakfast Recipes

Cheesy Egg Bites

Serves:2

Cooking Time: 30 Minutes

Ingredients:

- Nonstick cooking spray
- 3 large eggs
- 2 tablespoons milk
- ¼ teaspoon salt
- ¼ teaspoon black pepper
- ¼ chopped frozen broccoli florets
- ⅓ cup shredded cheese, divided

Directions:

1. Spray the 7 cavities of an egg bite mold with cooking spray.
2. In a small bowl, whisk together the eggs, milk, salt, and pepper.
3. Add the frozen broccoli and half of the cheese, and stir to combine.
4. Evenly pour or spoon the egg mixture into the prepared egg bite mold and top with the remaining cheese. Cover with the egg bite mold lid.
5. Place a trivet in the bottom of the Instant Pot, then pour in 1½ cups water. Place the filled egg bite mold on the trivet.
6. Lock the lid in place. Select Pressure Cook and adjust the pressure to High and the time to 10 minutes. After cooking, let the pressure release naturally for 5 minutes, then quick release any remaining pressure.
7. Once the float valve drops, open the lid and carefully remove the mold from the Instant Pot.
8. Let the egg bites cool for 5 minutes before removing from the mold. Serve warm.

Cheesy Egg And Bacon Muffins

Serves:4

Cooking Time: 8 Mins

Ingredients:

- 4 cooked bacon slices, crumbled
- 4 tbsps. shredded Cheddar cheese
- ¼ tsp. salt
- 1 green onion, chopped
- 4 eggs, beaten
- 1½ cups water

Directions:

1. In a bowl, mix the eggs with cheese, bacon, onion and salt, and whisk well. Pour the egg mixture evenly into four muffin cups.
2. Add 1½ cups water and steamer basket to the Instant Pot. Place the muffin cups in the basket.
3. Lock the lid. Select the Manual mode and set the cooking time for 8 minutes at High Pressure.
4. Once cooking is complete, do a quick pressure release. Carefully open the lid.
5. Divide the muffins between plates and serve warm.

Breakfast Arugula Salad

Serves:6

Cooking Time: 15 Mins

Ingredients:

- 2 blood oranges, peeled and sliced
- 2 cups water
- 4 oz. arugula
- 1 tsp. sunflower oil
- 1 cup kamut grains, soaked

Directions:

1. In the Instant Pot, combine the kamut grains with sunflower oil and water, and whisk well.
2. Lock the lid. Select the Manual mode and set the cooking time for 15 minutes at High Pressure.
3. Once cooking is complete, do a natural pressure release for 10 minutes, then release any remaining pressure. Carefully open the lid.
4. Drain the kamut grains and transfer to a large bowl. Add the arugula and oranges, and toss well. Serve immediately.

Fruit Yogurt

Serves:4

Cooking Time: 8 Hours

Ingredients:

- 3 cups milk
- 1 tbsp. vanilla bean paste
- 1 cup Greek yogurt
- 1 cup puréed fruit of your choice
- ¼ cup sugar

Directions:

1. Pour the milk into the Instant Pot.
2. Lock the lid. Set to the Adjust mode, then

pasteurize the milk for 45 minutes.
3. Once the pasteurizing is complete, perform a natural pressure release. Carefully open the lid.
4. Pour in the vanilla bean paste and Greek yogurt.
5. Lock the lid. Set to Yogurt mode, then set the timer for 8 hours at High pressure.
6. Once the timer goes off, perform a natural pressure release for 10 minutes, then release any remaining pressure. Carefully open the lid.
7. Pour the yogurt in a jar or a glass, then put in the refrigerator to chill for at least 1 hour.
8. Remove the yogurt from the refrigerator and mix in the puréed fruits and sugar before serving.

Celeriac And Bacon Mix

Serves:6

Cooking Time: 10 Mins

Ingredients:

- 2 tbsps. chicken stock
- 2 tsps. dried parsley
- 4 oz. shredded Cheddar cheese
- 3 bacon strips
- 2 lbs. peeled and cubed celeriac

Directions:

1. Set the Instant Pot to Sauté and cook the bacon for 2 minutes.
2. Add the parsley, celeriac and stock, and stir.
3. Lock the lid. Select the Manual mode and cook for 6 minutes at High Pressure.
4. Once cooking is complete, do a quick pressure release. Carefully open the lid.
5. Add the cheese and keep stirring until melted. Serve warm.

Monkey Bread

Serves: 2

Cooking Time: 20 Minutes

Ingredients:

- Nonstick Cooking Spray
- 3 Tablespoons Granulated Sugar
- ¼ Teaspoon Ground Cinnamon
- 1 (7.5-Ounce) Container Canned Biscuits
- 2 Tablespoons Butter, Melted
- ¼ Cup Packed Light Brown Sugar

Directions:

1. Spray a 3-Cup Bundt Pan (Or Other Nonstick Round Pan) With Cooking Spray.
2. In a Small Bowl, Mix The Granulated Sugar And Cinnamon Together.
3. Open The Can Of Biscuits And Cut Each Biscuit Into Four Pieces.
4. Dunk Each Piece Into The Cinnamon-Sugar Mixture And Roll To Coat. Place In The Prepared Pan.
5. In a Small Bowl, Stir Together The Melted Butter And Brown Sugar. Drizzle The Mixture Over The Biscuit Pieces. Cover The Pan Tightly With Aluminum Foil.
6. Place a Trivet In The Bottom Of The Instant Pot, Then Pour In 1½ Cups Water. Place The Pan On The Trivet.
7. Lock The Lid In Place. Select Pressure Cook And Adjust The Pressure To High And The Time To 20 Minutes. After Cooking, Move The Steam Release Handle To Venting And Quick Release The Pressure.
8. Once The Float Valve Drops, Open The Lid And Carefully Remove The Pan From The Instant Pot.
9. Let The Pan Sit For 10 Minutes, Then Invert Onto a Plate. Serve Warm.
10. Per Serving: Calories: 607; Carbohydrates: 95g; Fat: 23g; Fiber: 1g; Protein: 7g; Sugar: 53g; Sodium: 839mg

Breakfast Cobbler

Serves: 2

Cooking Time: 15 Mins

Ingredients:

- 2 tbsps. honey
- ¼ cup shredded coconut
- 1 plum, pitted and chopped
- 3 tbsps. coconut oil, divided
- 1 apple, cored and chopped

Directions:

1. In the Instant Pot, combine the plum with apple, half of the coconut oil, and honey, and blend well.
2. Lock the lid. Select the Manual mode and cook for 10 minutes at High Pressure.
3. Once cooking is complete, do a quick pressure release. Carefully open the lid.
4. Transfer the mixture to bowls and clean your Instant Pot.
5. Set your Instant Pot to Sauté and heat the remaining coconut oil. Add the coconut, stir, and toast for 5 minutes.
6. Sprinkle the coconut over fruit mixture and serve.

Swiss Chard Salad

Serves:4

Cooking Time: 12 Mins

Ingredients:

- ¼ tsp. red pepper flakes
- 1 bunch Swiss chard, sliced
- ¼ cup toasted pine nuts
- 1 tbsp. balsamic vinegar
- 2 tbsps. olive oil

Directions:

1. Set your Instant Pot to Sauté and heat the olive oil.
2. Add the chard, stir, and cook for 2 minutes until tender.
3. Add pepper flakes and vinegar and stir well.
4. Lock the lid. Select the Steam mode and cook for 3 minutes at High Pressure.
5. Sprinkle with the pine nuts and divide into bowls to serve.

Millet And Oats Porridge

Serves:8

Cooking Time: 13 Mins

Ingredients:

- 2 cored and chopped apples
- ½ cup rolled oats
- 3 cups water
- ½ tsp. ginger powder
- 1 cup mille

Directions:

1. Set the Instant Pot to Sauté and add the millet. Stir and toast for 3 minutes.
2. Add the oats, water, ginger and apples to the Instant Pot, and whisk to combine.
3. Lock the lid. Select the Manual mode and cook for 10 minutes at High Pressure.
4. Once cooking is complete, do a natural pressure release for 7 minutes, then release any remaining pressure. Carefully open the lid.
5. Stir the porridge again and ladle into bowls to serve.

Veggie Quiche

Serves:6

Cooking Time: 20 Mins

Ingredients:

- ½ cup milk
- 1 red bell pepper, chopped
- 2 green onions, chopped
- Salt, to taste
- 8 whisked eggs
- 1 cup water

Directions:

1. In a bowl, combine the whisked eggs with milk, bell pepper, onions and salt, and stir well. Pour the egg mixture into a pan.
2. In your Instant Pot, add the water and trivet. Place the pan on the trivet and cover with tin foil.
3. Lock the lid. Select the Manual mode and cook for 20 minutes at High Pressure.
4. Once cooking is complete, do a quick pressure release. Carefully open the lid.
5. Slice the quiche and divide between plates to serve.

Pomegranate Porridge

Serves:4

Cooking Time: 6 Mins

Ingredients:

- 2 pomegranates seeds
- 2 tbsps. sugar
- 2 cups shredded coconut
- 1 cup pomegranate juice
- 2 cup water

Directions:

1. In the Instant Pot, combine the coconut with water and pomegranate juice, and whisk well.
2. Lock the lid. Select the Manual mode and cook for 3 minutes at High Pressure.
3. Once cooking is complete, do a natural pressure release for 5 minutes, then release any remaining pressure. Carefully open the lid.
4. Add the pomegranate seeds and sugar and give a good stir. Ladle into bowls and serve warm.

French Eggs

Serves:4

Cooking Time: 8 Mins

Ingredients:

- ¼ tsp. salt
- 4 bacon slices
- 1 tbsp. olive oil
- 4 tbsps. chopped chives
- 4 eggs
- 1½ cups water

Directions:

1. Grease 4 ramekins with a drizzle of oil and crack an egg into each ramekin.

2. Add a bacon slice on top and season with salt. Sprinkle the chives on top.
3. Add 1½ cups water and steamer basket to your Instant Pot. Transfer the ramekins to the basket.
4. Lock the lid. Select the Manual mode and set the cooking time for 8 minutes at High Pressure.
5. Once cooking is complete, do a quick pressure release. Carefully open the lid.
6. Serve your baked eggs immediately.

Western Omelet

Serves:4

Cooking Time: 30 Mins

Ingredients:

- ½ cup half-and-half
- 4 chopped spring onions
- 6 whisked eggs
- ¼ tsp. salt
- 8 oz. bacon, chopped
- 1½ cups water

Directions:

1. Place the steamer basket in the Instant Pot and pour in 1½ cups water.
2. In a bowl, combine the eggs with half-and-half, bacon, spring onions and salt, and whisk well. Pour the egg mixture into a soufflé dish and transfer to the steamer basket.
3. Lock the lid. Select the Steam mode and cook for 30 minutes at High Pressure.
4. Once cooking is complete, do a quick pressure release. Carefully open the lid.
5. Allow to cool for 5 minutes before serving.

Eggs And Bacon Breakfast Risotto

Serves:2

Cooking Time: 12 Mins

Ingredients:

- 1½ cups chicken stock
- 2 poached eggs
- 2 tbsps. grated Parmesan cheese
- 3 chopped bacon slices
- ¾ cup Arborio rice

Directions:

1. Set your Instant Pot to Sauté and add the bacon and cook for 5 minutes until crispy, stirring occasionally.
2. Carefully stir in the rice and let cook for an additional 1 minute.
3. Add the chicken stock and stir well.
4. Lock the lid. Select the Manual mode and set the cooking time for 6 minutes at Low Pressure.
5. Once cooking is complete, do a quick pressure release. Carefully open the lid.
6. Add the Parmesan cheese and keep stirring until melted. Divide the risotto between two plates. Add the eggs on the side and serve immediately.

Ham And Spinach Frittata

Serves:8

Cooking Time: 10 Mins

Ingredients:

- 1 cup diced ham
- 2 cups chopped spinach
- 8 eggs, beaten
- ½ cup coconut milk
- 1 onion, chopped

- 1 tsp. salt

Directions:

1. Put all the ingredients into the Instant Pot. Stir to mix well.
2. Lock the lid. Set to Manual mode, then set the timer for 10 minutes at High Pressure.
3. Once the timer goes off, perform a natural pressure release for 5 minutes. Carefully open the lid.
4. Transfer the frittata on a plate and serve immediately.

Hard-"boiled" Eggs

Serves:6

Cooking Time: 6 Minutes

Ingredients:

- 1 cup water
- 6 large eggs

Directions:

1. Add water to the Instant Pot and insert steamer basket. Place eggs in basket. Lock lid.
2. Press the Manual or Pressure Cook button and adjust time to 6 minutes. When timer beeps, quick-release pressure until float valve drops. Unlock lid.
3. Create an ice bath by adding 1 cup ice and 1 cup water to a medium bowl. Transfer eggs to ice bath to stop the cooking process.
4. Peel eggs. Slice each egg directly onto a plate. Serve immediately.

Super Thick Cashew And Almond Milk Yogurt

Serves:4

Cooking Time: 8 Hours

Ingredients:

- ⅓ cup raw cashews
- 2 tbsps. arrowroot powder
- 4 cups almond milk
- ¼ cup yogurt with live culture
- 1 tbsp. maple syrup

Directions:

1. Combine the cashews, arrowroot powder, and almond milk in a food processor. Process until the mixture in creamy and smooth.
2. Pour the mixture in a saucepan and simmer for 5 minutes over medium heat. Keep stirring.
3. Turn off the heat and allow to cool.
4. Pour the mixture into the Instant Pot, then mix in the yogurt.
5. Lock the lid. Set to the Yogurt mode, then set the timer for 8 hours at High Pressure.
6. When the timer goes off, perform a natural pressure release for 10 minutes, then release any remaining pressure. Carefully open the lid.
7. Pour the yogurt in four mason jars, then put them in the refrigerator to chill for at least an hour.
8. Remove the jars from the refrigerator. Drizzle the yogurt with maple syrup and serve chilled

Zucchini Toast

Serves:2

Cooking Time: 8 Mins

Ingredients:

- ½ zucchini, sliced
- ¼ tsp. black pepper
- 1 tbsp. olive oil
- ½ tsp. salt
- 4 whole-grain bread slices, toasted

Directions:

1. In a bowl, toss the zucchini slices with salt. Set aside.
2. Select the Sauté mode on the Instant Pot and heat the olive oil.
3. Add the zucchini slices and sauté for about 6 minutes until softened, stirring occasionally. Season with black pepper.
4. Divide the zucchini slices evenly among bread slices and serve warm.

Turkey Breast And Avocado Breakfast

Serves:4

Cooking Time: 7 Mins

Ingredients:

- 4 whisked eggs
- 4 avocado slices
- 2 tbsps. olive oil
- 2 tbsps. vegetable stock
- 4 cooked turkey breast slices

Directions:

1. Set the Instant Pot to Sauté and heat the olive oil.
2. Add the turkey and brown for 2 minutes, then transfer to a plate.
3. Add the eggs and vegetable stock to the pot and whisk well.
4. Lock the lid. Select the Manual mode and cook for 5 minutes at High Pressure.
5. Once cooking is complete, do a quick pressure release. Carefully open the lid.
6. Divide the eggs and avocado slices next to turkey breast slices and serve

Cheesy Cauliflower Bowls

Serves:6

Cooking Time: 4 Mins

Ingredients:

- 1 tbsps. chopped parsley
- ½ cup vegetable stock
- 3 tbsps. olive oil
- 1 head cauliflower, cut into florets
- ⅓ cup grated Parmesan cheese

Directions:

1. In a bowl, combine the olive oil with cauliflower florets, and toss well.
2. Transfer to the Instant Pot and add stock.
3. Lock the lid. Select the Manual mode and set the cooking time for 4 minutes at High Pressure.
4. Once cooking is complete, do a quick pressure release. Carefully open the lid.
5. Add the parsley and Parmesan cheese, and stir to combine. Serve immediately

Pasta & Rice Recipes

Pasta & Rice Recipes

Green Cabbage And Tomatoes Side Dish

Serves: 4

Cooking Time: 5 Minutes

Ingredients:

- 15 oz. chopped canned tomatoes
- 3 tbsps. olive oil
- ½ cup chopped yellow onion
- 1 green cabbage head, chopped
- 2 tsps. turmeric powder

Directions:

1. Set the Instant Pot to Sauté and heat the olive oil. Add onion, stir, and cook for 2 minutes.
2. Add cabbage, tomatoes and turmeric, stir.
3. Lock the lid. Select the Manual mode, then set the timer for 4 minutes at High Pressure.
4. Once the timer goes off, perform a quick release. Carefully open the lid.
5. Divide between plates and serve as a side dish.

Family Truffle Popcorn

Serves: 4

Cooking Time: 15 Minutes

Ingredients:

- 1 stick butter
- 1 cup popcorn kernels
- 1 tablespoon truffle oil
- 1/4 cup parmesan cheese, grated
- Sea salt, to taste

Directions:

1. Press the "Sauté" button and melt the butter. Stir until it begins to simmer.
2. Stir in the popcorn kernels and cover. When the popping slows down, press the "Cancel" button.
3. Now, add the truffle oil, parmesan, and sea salt. Toss to combine and serve immediately.

Sweet Pearl Onion Mix

Serves: 4

Cooking Time: 5 Minutes

Ingredients:

- 4 tbsps. balsamic vinegar
- 1 tbsp. sugar
- 1 lb. pearl onions
- ½ cup water
- ¼ tsp. salt

Directions:

1. In the Instant Pot, mix pearl onions with salt, water, vinegar and sugar, stir.
2. Lock the lid. Select the Manual mode, then set the timer for 5 minutes on Low Pressure.
3. Once the timer goes off, perform a quick release. Carefully open the lid.
4. Toss onions again, divide them between plates and serve as a side dish.

Creamy Spinach

Serves: 4

Cooking Time: 6 Minutes

Ingredients:

- Ground nutmeg
- 10 oz. spinach, roughly chopped
- 2 shallots, chopped
- 2 cups heavy cream
- 2 tbsps. butter

Directions:

1. Set the Instant Pot to Sauté, add butter, melt it, add shallots, stir and cook for 2 minutes.
2. Add spinach, stir, and cook for 30 seconds more.
3. Add cream and nutmeg, stir.
4. Lock the lid. Select the Manual mode, then set the timer for 3 minutes at High Pressure.
5. Once the timer goes off, perform a quick release. Carefully open the lid.
6. Divide everything between plates and serve as a side dish.

Easy Jasmine Rice

Serves: 4-6

Cooking Time: 25 Minutes

Ingredients:

- 2 cups jasmine rice
- 2 cups water
- 2 tsp olive oil
- ½ tsp salt

Directions:

1. Rinse the rice well.
2. Transfer the rice to the Instant Pot. Add the water, oil and salt and stir.
3. Close and secure the lid. Select MANUAL

and cook at HIGH pressure for 4 minutes.
4. Once timer goes off, allow to Naturally Release for 10 minutes, then release the remaining pressure manually. Open the lid.
5. Fluff the rice with a fork and serve.

Yogurt Chicken Pilaf With Quinoa

Serves: 2-4

Cooking Time: 60 Minutes

Ingredients:

- 1 lb chicken breasts, boneless, skinless
- 1 cup quinoa
- 2 cups chicken broth
- Salt and black pepper to taste
- Greek yogurt for topping

Directions:

1. Add chicken and broth to the pot and seal the lid. Cook on Poultry for 15 minutes on High. Do a quick release and remove the chicken. Add quinoa and seal the lid. Cook on Rice mode for 8 minutes on High. Cut the chicken meat into bite-sized pieces and place in a large bowl. To the cooker, do a quick release. Stir in chicken, to warm, season with black pepper. and top with greek yogurt.

Hazelnut Brown Rice Pilaf

Serves: 4

Cooking Time: 35 Minutes

Ingredients:

- 2 tbsp olive oil
- ¼ cup hazelnuts, toasted and chopped
- 1 cup brown rice
- 2 cups vegetable broth
- Salt and black pepper to taste

Directions:

1. Place the rice, vegetable broth, olive oil, and salt in your Instant Pot and stir. Seal the lid, select Manual, and cook for 25 minutes on High. Once ready, allow a natural release for 10 minutes and unlock the lid. Using a fork, fluff the rice. Top with hazelnuts and serve.

Sweet Coconut Rice

Serves: 2-4

Cooking Time: 30 Minutes

Ingredients:

- 1 cup Thai sweet rice
- 1½ cups water
- ½ can full-fat coconut milk
- 2 tbsp sugar
- ½ tsp salt

Directions:

1. Add the rice and water to the Instant Pot, stir.
2. Close and secure the lid. Select MANUAL and cook at HIGH pressure for 3 minutes.
3. Once cooking is complete, use a Natural Release for 10 minutes, then release any remaining pressure manually.
4. Meanwhile, heat coconut milk, sugar, and salt in a saucepan.
5. When the sugar has melted, remove from the heat.
6. Open the pot and add the coconut milk mixture, stir to combine.
7. Put the lid back on and let it rest 5-10 minutes. Serve.

Haricots Verts Side Salad

Serves: 4

Cooking Time: 8 Minutes

Ingredients:

- 4 oz. pancetta, chopped
- Black pepper, to taste
- ½ cup chicken stock
- ½ cup sliced dates
- 2 lbs. haricot verts

Directions:

1. Set the Instant Pot to Sauté, add pancetta, stir and cook for 3 minutes.
2. Add haricot verts, dates and black pepper, stir and cook for 2 minutes more.
3. Stir in the stock.
4. Lock the lid. Select the Manual mode, then set the timer for 3 minutes on High Pressure.
5. Once the timer goes off, perform a quick release. Carefully open the lid.
6. Set in serving bowls and enjoy as a side dish.

Chestnut Mushrooms

Serves: 4

Cooking Time: 10 Minutes

Ingredients:

- 2 lbs. halved mushrooms
- ½ cup vegetable soup
- 1 tsp. Worcestershire sauce
- 1 cup halved jarred chestnuts
- 6 bacon slices, chopped

Directions:

1. Set the Instant Pot to Sauté, add bacon, stir and cook for 5 minutes on both sides.
2. Stir in the chestnuts and sauté for 1 more minute.
3. Add mushrooms, Worcestershire sauce and soup, stir.
4. Lock the lid. Select the Manual mode, then set the timer for 8 minutes at High Pressure.
5. Once the timer goes off, perform a quick release. Carefully open the lid.
6. Enjoy as a side dish.

Radishes Side Salad

Serves: 3

Cooking Time: 8 Minutes

Ingredients:

- 2 chopped bacon slices
- ½ cup veggie stock
- 2 tbsps. sour cream
- 1 tbsp. chopped green onions
- 7 oz. halved red radishes

Directions:

1. Set the Instant Pot to Sauté, add bacon, stir and cook for 6 minutes on both sides.
2. Add radishes and stock, stir.

3. Lock the lid. Select the Manual mode, then set the timer for 4 minutes at High Pressure.
4. Once the timer goes off, perform a quick release. Carefully open the lid.
5. Add sour cream and green onions, stir.
6. Lock the lid, then set the timer for 2 minutes.
7. Divide between plates and serve as a side dish.

Cauliflower And Pineapple Rice

Serves: 4-6

Cooking Time: 40 Minutes

Ingredients:

- 2 tsp extra virgin olive oil
- 4 cups water
- 2 cups jasmine rice
- 1 cauliflower, florets separated and chopped
- ½ pineapple, peeled and chopped
- Salt and ground black pepper to taste

Directions:

1. Combine all of the ingredients in the Instant Pot and stir to combine.
2. Close and secure the lid. Select the MANUAL setting and set the cooking time for 20 minutes at LOW pressure.
3. Once pressure cooking is complete, let Naturally Release for 10 minutes, then quick release remaining pressure.
4. Carefully open the pot. Fluff the dish with the rice spatula or fork. Serve.

Corn On The Cob With Cilantro Butter

Serves: 6

Cooking Time: 15 Minutes

Ingredients:

- 6 large ears corn, husked and halved
- 6 tablespoons butter, softened
- 2 heaping tablespoons cilantro, chopped
- 1 teaspoon paprika
- Sea salt and ground black pepper, to taste

Directions:

1. Place 1 cup of water and a metal trivet in your Instant Pot. Now, lower the corn onto the trivet.
2. Secure the lid. Choose the "Manual" mode and cook for 6 minutes at High pressure. Once cooking is complete, use a quick pressure release; carefully remove the lid.
3. Press the "Sauté" button and melt the butter; add the cilantro, paprika, salt, and black pepper to the melted butter.
4. Pour the cilantro butter over the steamed corn and enjoy!

Almond & Raisin Quinoa

Serves: 4

Cooking Time: 15 Minutes

Ingredients:

- 1 cup quinoa
- 1 cup raisins, soaked
- ½ cup slivered almonds
- ¼ cup salted sunflower seeds

Directions:

1. Place quinoa and 2 cups water in your Instant Pot. Seal the lid, select Manual, and

cook for 10 minutes on High pressure. Once done, perform a quick pressure release. Stir in sunflower seeds, almonds, and raisins. Serve.

Mexican-style Salsa Rice

Serves: 4

Cooking Time: 35 Minutes

Ingredients:

- 1 cup brown rice
- 1 cup chicken broth
- 1 cup chunky salsa
- 1 cup Cotija cheese, shredded

Directions:

1. Add the brown rice, chicken broth, salsa, oregano, salt, and black pepper to the inner pot.
2. Secure the lid. Choose the "Manual" mode and cook for 22 minutes at High pressure. Once cooking is complete, use a natural pressure release for 10 minutes; carefully remove the lid.
3. Divide between serving bowls and serve with shredded cheese. Enjoy!

Kidney Beans And Corn Side Dish

Serves: 2

Cooking Time: 10 Minutes

Ingredients:

- ½ tsp. chili powder
- 1½ cups chicken stock
- 1 cup cooked kidney beans
- ½ cup corn
- 1 small red onion, chopped

Directions:

1. In the Instant Pot, mix beans with corn, onion, chili powder and stock, stir.
2. Lock the lid. Select the Manual mode, then set the timer for 10 minutes at High Pressure.
3. Once the timer goes off, perform a quick release. Carefully open the lid.
4. Enjoy the side dish!

Pasta With Meat Sauce

Serves: 4

Cooking Time: 25 Minutes

Ingredients:

- 1 tsp olive oil
- 1 lb ground beef
- 8 oz dried pasta
- 1½ cup water
- 24 oz pasta sauce
- Italian seasoning to taste
- Salt and ground black pepper to taste

Directions:

1. Preheat the Instant Pot by selecting SAUTÉ. Add and heat the oil.
2. Add the ground beef and cook until all the meat is browned, stirring occasionally.
3. Add the pasta, water and sauce, stir well.
4. Press the CANCEL key to stop the SAUTÉ function.
5. Close and lock the lid. Select MANUAL and cook at HIGH pressure for 7 minutes.
6. When the timer beeps, use a Quick Release. Carefully unlock the lid.
7. Sprinkle with Italian seasoning, salt and pepper to taste. Stir and serve.

Arborio Rice Side Salad

Serves: 4

Cooking Time: 4 Minutes

Ingredients:

- 1 bunch basil, chopped
- 4 cups water
- 2 cups Arborio rice
- ¼ tsp. salt
- 1 cup pitted and sliced black olives in oil

Directions:

1. In the Instant Pot, mix rice with water.
2. Lock the lid. Select the Manual mode, then set the timer for 20 minutes at Low Pressure.
3. Once the timer goes off, perform a natural release for 10 minutes, then release any remaining pressure. Carefully open the lid.
4. Drain and transfer to a salad bowl.
5. Add a pinch of salt, olives and basil, toss well, divide between plates and serve as a side salad.

Coconut Cherry Steel Cut Oats

Serves: 4

Cooking Time: 15 Minutes

Ingredients:

- 1 cup cherries, pitted and halved
- 1 cup steel cut oats
- 1 cup coconut milk
- 2 cups water
- ½ tsp vanilla extract

Directions:

1. Place cherries, oats, milk, water, and vanilla extract in your Instant Pot. Seal the lid, select Manual, and cook for 3 minutes on High pressure. Once ready, allow a natural release for 10 minutes and unlock the lid. Serve immediately.

Movie Night Popcorn

Serves: 4

Cooking Time:15 Minutes

Ingredients:

- 1/4 cup parmesan cheese, grated
- 1 cup popcorn kernels
- 1 tablespoon truffle oil
- 1 stick butter
- Sea salt, to taste

Directions:

1. Press the "Sauté" button and melt the butter. Stir until it begins to simmer.
2. Stir in the popcorn kernels and cover. When the popping slows down, press the "Cancel" button.
3. Now, add the truffle oil, parmesan, and sea salt. Toss to combine and serve immediately.

Poultry Recipes

Poultry Recipes

Instant Bbq Chicken Wings

Serves: 6

Cooking Time: 15 Minutes

Ingredients:

- 2 lbs. chicken wings
- ¾ cup barbecue sauce of your choice
- 2 tablespoons seasoned salt1 cup cold water
- ¼ cup hot sauce

Directions:

1. Place chicken wings in a medium-sized bowl and add seasoned salt to it.
2. Toss the wings in the bowl to add more flavour.
3. Put the seasoned chicken wings in an instant pot and add the barbecue sauce to it.
4. Add 1 cup of water to the pot then secure the lid.
5. Select the 'manual' function on the pressure cooker and set to high pressure for 10 minutes
6. Once it beeps, release the steam carefully with 'quick release'.
7. Remove the lid and let the wings stay for 2 minutes.
8. Now stir in the hot sauce with the chicken wings to enrich their flavour.
9. Serve.

Chicken Curry

Serves: 6

Cooking Time: 15 Minutes

Ingredients:

- 2 cups freshly squeezed coconut milk
- 1½ lbs. boneless chicken breasts
- 2 cups chopped tomatoes
- 2 tbsps. curry powder
- 1 ginger
- Salt and pepper, to taste

Directions:

1. Press the Sauté button on the Instant Pot. Add the chicken breasts and cook for 3 minutes until lightly golden. Season with salt and pepper.
2. Stir in the curry powder and continue cooking for 2 minutes more. Add the remaining ingredients and whisk well.
3. Press the Poultry button and set the cooking time for 10 minutes.
4. Once cooking is complete, do a natural pressure release for 6 minutes, then release any remaining pressure. Carefully open the lid.
5. Cool for 5 minutes and serve on plates.

Turkey With Broccoli & Carrots

Serves:4

Cooking Time: 15 Minutes

Ingredients:

- 1 cup carrots, chopped
- 1 lb turkey breast, sliced
- 1 cup broccoli florets
- 1 tbsp butter
- Salt and pepper, to taste
- 1 cup water

Directions:

1. Add water and a trivet to IP. Put carrots and broccoli on top. Seal the lid, press Steam, and cook for 3 minutes at High. Quick release the pressure, and set aside. Melt butter on Sauté and stir-fry turkey for 8 minutes. Season to taste, and pour over the veggies to serve.

Chicken Yogurt Salsa

Serves: 4

Cooking Time: 15 Minutes

Ingredients:

- 1 medium jar salsa
- ½ cup water
- 1 cup plain Greek yogurt
- 4 chicken breasts

Directions:

1. Add all the ingredients to the Instant Pot. Using a spatula, gently stir to combine well.
2. Lock the lid. Select the Poultry mode and set the cooking time for 15 minutes at High Pressure.
3. Once cooking is complete, do a natural pres-sure release for 8 minutes, then release any remaining pressure. Carefully open the lid.
4. Transfer the cooked mixture to a salad bowl and serve warm.

Shredded Chicken Breast

Serves: 4

Cooking Time: 30 Minutes

Ingredients:

- 1.5-2 lbs boneless chicken breasts
- ½ tsp ground black pepper
- ½ tsp garlic salt
- ½ cup chicken broth

Directions:

1. Season all sides of the chicken with the black pepper and salt.
2. Add the chicken breasts to the Instant Pot and pour the chicken broth.
3. Close and lock the lid. Select MANUAL and cook at HIGH pressure for 8 minutes.
4. Once cooking is complete, use a Natural Release for 10 minutes, then release any remaining pressure manually.
5. Remove the chicken from the pot and shred it with 2 forks. Serve.

Soft-boiled Eggs

Serves: 2

Cooking Time: 10 Minutes

Ingredients:

- 4 eggs
- 1 cup water
- 2 English muffins, toasted
- Salt and ground black pepper to taste

Directions:

1. Prepare the Instant Pot by adding the water to the pot and insert a steamer basket.
2. Put the eggs in the basket.
3. Close and lock the lid. Select the STEAM setting and set the cooking time for 4 minutes.
4. When the timer goes off, use a Quick Release. Carefully unlock the lid.
5. Transfer the eggs to the bowl of cold water. Wait 2-3 minutes.
6. Peel the eggs. Serve one egg per half of toasted English muffin.
7. Sprinkle with salt and pepper to taste.

Shredded Chicken With Marinara

Serves: 4-6

Cooking Time: 40 Minutes

Ingredients:

- 4 lbs chicken breasts
- ½ cup chicken broth
- ½ tsp black pepper
- 1 tsp salt
- 2 cups marinara sauce

Directions:

1. Add the chicken breasts, broth, pepper, and salt to the Instant Pot, stir well.
2. Close and lock the lid. Select MANUAL and cook at HIGH pressure for 20 minutes.
3. Once pressure cooking is complete, use a Quick Release. Unlock and carefully open the lid.
4. Shred the chicken in the pot.
5. Select the SAUTÉ setting. Add the marinara sauce and simmer for 5 minutes.
6. Serve with cooked rice, potato, peas or green salad.

Instant Pot Pesto Chicken

Serves: 4

Cooking Time: 10 Minutes

Ingredients:

- 4 chicken breasts
- ¼ cup extra virgin olive oil
- Salt and pepper, to taste
- 2 cups basil leaves
- 5 sun-dried tomatoes
- 1 cup water, if needed

Directions:

1. Put the basil leaves, olive oil, and tomatoes in the food processor until smooth. Season with salt and people to taste. Add a cup of water if needed.
2. Place the chicken in the Instant Pot. Pour the sauce over the chicken.
3. Lock the lid. Select the Manual mode and cook for 8 minutes at High Pressure.
4. Once cooking is complete, do a natural pressure release for 6 minutes, then release any remaining pressure. Carefully open the lid.
5. Transfer to a large plate and serve warm.

Chicken Breasts With Caraway Seeds

Serves:4

Cooking Time: 35 Minutes

Ingredients:

- 2 lb chicken breasts
- 1 cup celery, chopped
- 1 tbsp caraway seeds
- 1 carrot, chopped
- 2 ¼ cups vegetable stock
- Salt and black pepper to taste

Directions:

1. Chop the chicken into small pieces and place in your IP. Add the remaining ingredients and stir well to combine. Seal the lid and cook on Manual for 15 minutes at High. When ready, release pressure naturally for 10 minutes. Season with salt and pepper and serve.

Smoky Paprika Chicken

Serves: 6

Cooking Time: 15 Minutes

Ingredients:

- 2 tbsps. smoked paprika
- 2 lbs. chicken breasts
- Salt and pepper, to taste
- 1 tbsp. olive oil
- ½ cup water

Directions:

1. Press the Sauté button on the Instant Pot and heat the olive oil.
2. Stir in the chicken breasts and smoked paprika and cook for 3 minutes until lightly golden.

3. Season with salt and pepper and add ½ cup water.
4. Lock the lid. Select the Manual mode and cook for 12 minutes at High Pressure.
5. Once cooking is complete, do a natural pressure release for 8 minutes, then release any remaining pressure. Carefully open the lid.
6. Garnish with cilantro or scallions, if desired.

Flavorful Chicken With Lemongrass

Servings: 4

Cooking Time: 35 Minutes

Ingredients:

- 2 lemongrass stalks, chopped
- 2 garlic cloves, minced
- Salt and black pepper to taste
- 1 cup chicken broth
- 4 chicken breasts
- 1 lemon, juiced

Directions:

1. In your Instant Pot, combine lemongrass, garlic, salt, pepper, broth, and chicken. Seal the lid, select Pressure Cook, and set the time to 12 minutes. After cooking, perform a natural pressure release for 10 minutes. Unlock the lid. Select Sauté and remove chicken onto a plate. Take out the lemongrass and discard. Shred chicken into strands and return to sauce. Stir in lemon juice and cook for 5 minutes. Serve warm.

Chimichurri Chicken

Serves: 6

Cooking Time: 25 Minutes

Ingredients:

- 2 lb chicken breasts
- 1 cup chicken broth
- 1 tsp smoked paprika
- 1 tsp cumin
- Salt and black pepper to taste
- 2 cups chimichurri salsa

Directions:

1. Sprinkle chicken breasts with paprika, cumin, salt, and pepper. Place the chicken broth with chicken breasts in your Instant Pot. Seal the lid, select Manual, and cook for 15 minutes on High pressure. Once done, perform a quick pressure release and unlock the lid. Cut the chicken into slices and top with chimichurri sauce. Serve immediately.

Ginger Chicken Congee

Serves: 4

Cooking Time: 25 Minutes

Ingredients:

- 2 cups rice
- 8 medium chicken breasts
- 4 cups water
- 4-inch minced ginger piece
- 1 chicken stock cube
- Salt and pepper, to taste

Directions:

1. Add the rice, water, chicken breasts, chicken stock, and ginger to the Instant Pot. Season with salt and pepper.
2. Lock the lid. Select the Poultry mode and

set the cooking time for 25 minutes at High Pressure.
3. Once cooking is complete, do a natural pressure release for 10 minutes, then release any remaining pressure. Carefully open the lid. Serve warm.

Allspice Turkey Drumsticks With Beer

Serves: 2

Cooking Time: 20 Minutes

Ingredients:

- 1 lb. turkey drumsticks, boneless
- 1 (6-oz) bottle beer
- 1 carrot, sliced
- 1 small leek, sliced
- ¼ tsp. ground allspice
- Sea salt and freshly ground black pepper, to taste

Directions:

1. Place all the ingredients in the Instant Pot and stir well.
2. Lock the lid. Select the Manual mode and cook for 20 minutes at High Pressure.
3. Once cooking is complete, do a natural pressure release for 10 minutes, then release any remaining pressure. Carefully open the lid.
4. Remove from the pot and serve on a plate.

Lemon Garlic Chicken

Serves: 6

Cooking Time: 12 Minutes

Ingredients:

- 3 tbsps. olive oil, divided
- 2 tsps. dried parsley
- 6 chicken breasts
- 3 minced garlic cloves
- 1 tbsp. lemon juice
- Salt and pepper, to taste

Directions:

1. Mix together 2 tablespoons olive oil, chicken breasts, parsley, garlic cloves, and lemon juice in a large bowl. Place in the refrigerator to marinate for 1 hour.
2. Press the Sauté button on the Instant Pot and heat the remaining olive oil.
3. Cook the chicken breasts for 5 to 6 minutes per side until cooked through.
4. Allow to cool for 5 minutes before serving.

Bbq Chicken

Serves: 3

Cooking Time: 12 Minutes

Ingredients:

- ½ cup barbecue sauce
- 2 lbs. chicken breasts
- 1 cup water
- 2½ tbsps. honey
- ½ cup chopped onion
- Salt and pepper, to taste

Directions:

1. In the Instant Pot, add all the ingredients and stir well.
2. Lock the lid. Select the Manual mode and set the timer to 12 minutes at High Pressure.
3. Once cooking is complete, do a natural pressure release for 5 minutes, then release any remaining pressure. Carefully open the lid.
4. Cook for a few minutes to thicken the sauce. Serve warm.

Simple Sage Whole Chicken

Serves:4

Cooking Time: 35 Minutes

Ingredients:

- 1 (3-lb) whole chicken
- 2 tbsp olive oil
- Salt and black pepper to taste
- 2 fresh sage, chopped

Directions:

1. Season chicken all over with salt and pepper. Heat the oil on Sauté and cook the chicken until browned on all sides. Set aside and wipe clean the cooker. Insert a rack in your pressure cooker and pour in 1 cup of water. Lower the chicken onto the rack. Seal the lid, press Poultry and cook for 25 minutes at High. Once ready, do a quick pressure release. Let cool for a few minutes, slice, and sprinkle with sage to serve.

Mushroom Frittata

Serves: 2-4

Cooking Time: 20 Minutes

Ingredients:

- 4 beaten eggs
- 1 cup fresh mushrooms, chopped
- ¼ cup half-and-half
- Salt and freshly ground black pepper to taste
- 1 cup sharp cheddar cheese, shredded and divided
- 1 cup water

Directions:

1. In a medium bowl, combine the eggs, mushrooms, half-and-half, salt and pepper, and ½ cup cheese. Mix well.
2. Divide mixture into ½-pint wide mouth jars evenly and sprinkle with remaining cheese. Cover the jars with lids loosely.
3. Pour the water into the Instant Pot and insert a steamer trivet. Place the jars on top of trivet.
4. Close and lock the lid. Select the MANUAL setting and set the cooking time for 3 minutes at HIGH pressure.
5. Once pressure cooking is complete, use a Quick Release. Carefully unlock the lid. Serve.

Egg Muffins

Serves: 2

Cooking Time: 15 Minutes

Ingredients:

- 4 beaten eggs
- 4 bacon slices, cooked and crumbled
- 4 tbsp cheddar cheese, shredded
- 1 green onion, chopped
- A pinch of salt
- 1½ cups water

Directions:

1. In a medium bowl, whisk together eggs, bacon, cheese, onion and salt until combined.
2. Divide the mixture into muffin cups.
3. Pour the water into the Instant Pot and insert a steamer basket.
4. Place the muffin cups in the basket.
5. Close and lock the lid. Select MANUAL and cook at HIGH pressure for 8 minutes.
6. When the timer goes off, allow a 2 minutes rest time and then do a Quick Release.
7. Carefully unlock the lid. Remove the steamer basket with muffins from the pot. Serve.

Chinese Steamed Chicken

Serves:6

Cooking Time: 10 Mins

Ingredients:

- 1 tsp. grated ginger
- 1½ lbs. chicken thighs
- 1 tbsp. five-spice powder
- ¼ cup soy sauce
- 3 tbsps. sesame oil
- 1 cup water
- Salt and pepper, to taste

Directions:

1. In the Instant Pot, stir in all the ingredients.
2. Lock the lid. Select the Poultry mode and set the cooking time for 10 minutes at High Pressure.
3. Once cooking is complete, do a natural pressure release for 7 minutes, then release any remaining pressure. Carefully open the lid.
4. Serve the chicken thighs while warm.

Beef & Lamb, Pork Recipes

Beef & Lamb, Pork Recipes

Saucy Red Chili Pork

Servings: 4

Cooking Time: 35 Minutes

Ingredients:

- 1 lb pork loin
- ¼ cup red chili puree
- 1 cup chicken broth
- Salt and black pepper to taste
- 1 tsp dried rosemary

Directions:

1. In the inner pot of your Instant Pot, combine pork, red chili puree, broth, salt, pepper, and rosemary. Seal the lid, select Pressure Cook on High, and set the time to 15 minutes.
2. Once done, allow a natural release for 10 minutes. Shred pork with two forks, stir and adjust taste with salt and pepper. Serve with rice and bread dishes.

Ingredient Pork Chops

Serves: 2

Cooking Time: 25 Minutes

Ingredients:

- 2 tablespoons lemon pepper
- 2 pork chops, bone in
- ¼ cup apple juice

Directions:

1. Place all ingredients in the Instant Pot.
2. Close the lid and press the Meat/Stew button.
3. Adjust the cooking time to 25 minutes.
4. Do natural pressure release.

Asparagus Wrapped In Parma Ham

Serves: 4

Cooking Time: 15 Minutes

Ingredients:

- 1 lb asparagus, trimmed
- ½ lb Parma ham, thinly sliced
- 2 tbsp Parmesan cheese, grated

Directions:

1. Pour 1 cup of water in your Instant Pot and fit in a trivet. Wrap each asparagus spear with a ham slice and place on the trivet. Seal the lid, select Manual, and cook for 3 minutes on High pressure.
2. When over, allow a natural release for 5 minutes, then perform a quick pressure release, and unlock the lid. Transfer the wraps to a greased baking dish and sprinkle with the Parmesan cheese. Place under preheated broiler for about 4 minutes until the cheese is melted. Serve immediately.

German Sausages With Peppers And Onions

Servings:4

Cooking Time: 40 Minutes

Ingredients:

- 2 tablespoons vegetable oil
- 4 large German sausages, such as bratwurst
- 1 large onion, halved and cut into ¼-inch-thick slices
- 1 green bell pepper, seeded and cut into ¼-inch-thick rings
- 1 red bell pepper, seeded and cut into ¼-inch-thick rings
- ½ teaspoon kosher salt
- Freshly ground black pepper
- 1 bottle German-style lager

Directions:

1. Select Sauté, set the heat to Medium, and add the oil. When it shimmers, add the sausages. Brown them on one side for 3 to 4 minutes, then turn and brown the opposite side. Transfer the sausages to a plate and set aside.
2. Set the heat to High. Add the onion and stir. Cook for 4 to 5 minutes, until the onion starts to brown.
3. Add the bell peppers and cook for 1 to 2 minutes, stirring. Season with the salt and black pepper. Add the lager and bring to a boil for 2 minutes to evaporate some of the alcohol. Return the sausages to the pot.
4. Lock the lid into place. Select Pressure Cook or Manual; set the pressure to High and the time to 8 minutes.
5. After the cook time is complete, let the pressure release Naturally for 5 minutes, then Quick release any remaining pressure. Unlock and remove the lid.
6. Serve the sausages topped with the peppers and onions.

Sunday Pork Roast

Serves: 12

Cooking Time: 15 Minutes

Ingredients:

- 4 lbs. pork roast
- 1 tbsp. sea salt
- 4 tbsps. extra virgin olive oil
- 4 Chinese eggplants, rinsed, stem removed, and cut into ¼-inch slices
- 1 cup chicken stock

Directions:

1. On a clean work surface, rub the pork with salt.
2. Set the Instant Pot to Sauté mode. Add the olive oil to Instant Pot and heat until shimmering.
3. Add pork and brown for 3 minutes on all sides.
4. Add eggplant and stock.
5. Lock the lid. Set the pot to Manual setting and set the timer for 15 minutes at High Pressure.
6. Once cooking is complete, use a quick pressure release.
7. Carefully open the lid. Allow to cool for a few minutes. Transfer them on a large plate and serve immediately.

Instant Pot Ribs

Serves: 4

Cooking Time: 30 Minutes

Ingredients:

- ½ rack spare ribs
- Salt and pepper
- 1 cup beef stock
- 3 tablespoons Dijon mustard
- 3 tablespoons brown sugar

Directions:

1. Place all ingredients in the Instant Pot.
2. Close the lid and press the Meat/Stew button.
3. Adjust the cooking time to 30 minutes.
4. Do natural pressure release.

Savoy Cabbage With Pancetta

Serves:8

Cooking Time: 35 Minutes

Ingredients:

- 1 lb Savoy cabbage, chopped
- 8 pancetta slices, chopped
- 1 ½ cups vegetable broth
- 2 tbsp butter
- Salt and black pepper to taste

Directions:

1. Add pancetta slices in your IP, and cook for 5 minutes until crispy on Sauté. Stir in cabbage, salt, pepper, and butter. Seal the lid, hit Manual for 10 minutes at High. Release pressure naturally for 10 minutes.

Pork Coconut Curry

Serves: 6

Cooking Time: 35 Minutes

Ingredients:

- 3 tbsps. coconut oil
- 3 garlic cloves, minced
- 1 tbsp. garam masala
- 2 lbs. pork shoulders, sliced
- 1 cup freshly squeezed coconut milk
- Salt and pepper, to taste

Directions:

1. Press the Sauté button on the Instant Pot and heat the coconut oil until melted.
2. Add and sauté the garlic and garam masala until fragrant.
3. Add the pork and allow to sear on all sides for 3 minutes or until lightly browned.
4. Pour in the coconut milk. Sprinkle with salt and pepper.
5. Lock the lid. Press the Meat/Stew button and set the cooking time to 30 minutes at High pressure.
6. Once cooking is complete, perform a natural pressure release for 10 minutes, and then release any remaining pressure. Carefully open the lid.
7. Remove the pork from the pot and serve warm.

T-bone Steaks With Basil & Mustard

Serves: 4

Cooking Time: 1 Hour 35 Minutes

Ingredients:

- 1 lb T-bone steak (2 pieces)
- Salt and black pepper to taste
- 2 tbsp Dijon mustard
- ¼ cup oil
- ½ tsp dried basil, crushed

Directions:

1. Whisk together oil, mustard, salt, pepper, and basil. Brush each steak and Refrigerate for 1 hour. Meanwhile, insert the steamer tray in the instant pot.
2. Pour 3 cups of water and arrange the steaks on the tray. Seal the lid and cook on Steam mode for 25 minutes on High. Do a quick release and open the pot. Discard the liquid, remove the tray, and hit Sauté. Brown the steaks, one at the time, for 5 minutes, turning once.

Fried Rice With Sausage And Egg

Serves: 2

Cooking Time: 15 Minutes

Ingredients:

- 1 tsp. butter
- 2 oz. chorizo sausage, thinly sliced
- 2 large eggs, beaten
- 2 cups cooked rice
- 1 red bell pepper, chopped
- Salt and pepper, to taste

Directions:

1. Press Sauté on the Instant Pot. Heat the butter in the pot until melted.
2. Add the sausage and sauté for 2 to 3 minutes per side to evenly brown.
3. Add the beaten eggs and sauté for 2 to 3 minutes to scramble.
4. Add the rice and bell pepper. Sprinkle with salt and pepper. Sauté for 5 minutes; serve warm.

Barbecued Pork Ribs

Servings:x

Cooking Time: 45 Minutes

Ingredients:

- 1 pound country style pork ribs
- Coarse sea salt and freshly ground black pepper, to taste
- 1/2 teaspoon red pepper flakes
- 1/4 cup Marsala wine
- 1/4 cup chicken broth
- 1/2 cup BBQ sauce

Directions:

1. Place the pork ribs, salt, black pepper, red pepper, wine, and chicken broth in the inner pot.
2. Choose the "Meat/Stew" mode and cook for 35 minutes at High pressure. Once cooking is complete, use a quick pressure release; carefully remove the lid.
3. Transfer the pork ribs to a baking pan. Pour the BBQ sauce over the pork ribs and roast in the preheated oven at 425 °F for 6 to 8 minutes. Bon appétit!

Greek-style Cooked Pulled Pork

Serves:4

Cooking Time: 46 Minutes

Ingredients:

- 2 tbsp Greek seasoning
- 2 tbsp olive oil
- 1 jar sliced pepperoncini
- 2 lb pork tenderloin, fat trimmed
- 2 tbsp fresh dill, chopped

Directions:

1. Sprinkle pork with the Greek seasoning. Heat the olive oil on Sauté in the IP and brown the pork on all sides for 5-6 minutes. Pour the jar of pepperoncini peppers and ½ cup of water over the pork. Seal the lid, select Manual at High, and cook for 20 minutes. When ready, release the pressure naturally for 10 minutes. Remove the pork and shred using two forks. Return the shredded pork to cooker and stir. Serve sprinkled with fresh dill.

Shredded Pepper Steak

Serves: 6-8

Cooking Time: 1 Hour 30 Minutes

Ingredients:

- 3-4 lbs beef (cheap steak or roast cuts will all work)
- 1 tbsp garlic powder
- Red chili flakes to taste
- 1 jar (16 oz) mild pepper rings (banana peppers or pepperoncini)
- ½ cup salted beef broth

Directions:

1. Add beef to the Instant Pot and season with garlic powder and red chili.
2. Pour the pepper rings and broth into the pot, stir.
3. Close and lock the lid. Select the MANUAL setting and set the cooking time for 70 minutes at HIGH pressure.
4. Once cooking is complete, use a Natural Release for 10 minutes, then release any remaining pressure manually. Open the lid.
5. Shred the meat in the pot (or transfer to a plate) and stir. Serve.

Cheese Beef Taco Pie

Serves:4

Cooking Time: 20 Minutes

Ingredients:

- 1 package corn tortillas
- 1 packet of taco seasoning
- 1 lb ground beef
- 12 oz Colby cheese
- ¼ cup refried beans
- Salt and black pepper to taste

Directions:

1. Combine meat with the seasoning. Pour 1 cup of water in your IP and insert a trivet. Place 1 tortilla at the bottom of a baking pan and lay on the trivet. Top with beans, beef, and cheese. Top with another tortilla. Repeat until you've use up all ingredients. The final layer should be a tortilla. Seal the lid, and cook for 12 minutes on Manual at High. When ready, do a quick pressure release. Remove the pan and serve.

Green Onion Pork Frittata

Serves: 2-4

Cooking Time: 30 Minutes

Ingredients:

- 1 tbsp butter, melted
- 1 cup green onions, chopped
- 1 pound ground pork, chopped
- 6 eggs
- Salt and black pepper, to taste
- 1 cup water

Directions:

1. In a deep bowl, break the eggs and whisk until frothy. Mix in the onions and ground meat, and season with the salt and pepper. Grease a casserole dish with 1 tablespoon of melted butter. Pour the egg mixture into the dish.
2. Place a metal trivet in the pressure cooker and add 1 cup of water. Select Rice mode and cook for 25 minutes on High. Do a quick pressure release and serve immediately.

Parmesan Pork Chops

Serves: 4

Cooking Time: 20 Minutes

Ingredients:

- 1 tablespoon lard, at room temperature
- 4 pork chops, bone-in
- Sea salt and freshly ground black pepper, to taste
- 1/4 cup tomato puree
- 1 cup chicken bone broth
- 4 ounces parmesan cheese, preferably freshly grated

Directions:

1. Press the "Sauté" button and melt the lard. Sear the pork chops for 3 to 4 minutes per side. Season with salt and pepper.
2. Place the tomato puree and chicken broth in the inner pot.
3. Secure the lid. Choose the "Manual" mode and cook for 10 minutes at High pressure. Once cooking is complete, use a natural pressure release; carefully remove the lid.
4. Top with parmesan cheese and serve warm. Bon appétit!

Pork Chops In Cream Of Mushrooms

Serves:4

Cooking Time: 35 Minutes

Ingredients:

- 10 oz condensed cream of mushroom soup
- Salt and black pepper to taste
- 1 cup milk
- 4 boneless pork chops
- 1 tbsp ranch dressing

Directions:

1. Combine all the ingredients, except for the pork chops, in a mixing bowl. Place the chops into the IP, and pour mixture over. Pour in ½ cup of water. Seal the lid, select Manual at High, and cook for 10 minutes. When ready, release the pressure naturally for 10 minutes.

Plum Sauce Pork Chops

Serves: 2-4

Cooking Time: 20 Minutes

Ingredients:

- 4 pork chops
- 1 tsp cumin seeds
- Salt and black pepper to taste
- 2 cups firm plums, pitted and chopped
- 1 tbsp vegetable oil
- ¾ cup vegetable stock

Directions:

1. Sprinkle salt, cumin, and pepper on the pork chops. Set on Sauté and warm oil. Add the chops and cook for 3 to 5 minutes and set aside on a bowl. Arrange plum slices at the bottom of the cooker. Place pork chops on top of the plumes. Add any juice from the plate over the pork and apply stock around the edges. Seal lid and cook on High for 8 minutes. Do a quick Pressure release. Transfer pork chops to a serving plate and spoon over the plum sauce.

Carrot Casserole With Beef & Potato

Serves: 3

Cooking Time: 20 Minutes

Ingredients:

- 1 lb lean beef, with bones
- 2 carrots
- 1 potato, sliced
- 3 tbsp olive oil
- ½ tsp salt

Directions:

1. Mix all ingredients in the instant pot. Pour enough water to cover and seal the lid. Cook on High Pressure for 15 minutes. Do a quick release and serve hot.

Simple Roast Lamb

Serves: 4

Cooking Time: 40 Minutes

Ingredients:

- 2 lb lamb leg
- 1 tbsp garlic powder
- 3 tbsp extra virgin olive oil
- Salt and black pepper to taste
- 4 rosemary sprigs, chopped

Directions:

1. Grease the inner pot with oil. Rub the meat with salt, pepper, and garlic powder, and place in the instant pot. Pour enough water to cover and seal the lid. Cook on Meat/Stew for 30 minutes on High. Do a quick release. Make sure the meat is tender and falls off the bones. Top with cooking juices and rosemary.

Beans & Grains Recipes

Beans & Grains Recipes

Elegant Bean Purée

Servings:x

Cooking Time: 30 Minutes | Servings 4

Ingredients:

- 1 tablespoon canola oil
- 1/2 cup scallions, chopped
- 4 cloves garlic, smashed
- 1 ½ cups Adzuki beans
- 2 cups water
- 3 cups beef bone broth
- Sea salt and freshly ground black pepper, to taste
- 1 teaspoon paprika

Directions:

1. Press the "Sauté" button to preheat your Instant Pot. Then, heat the oil and cook the scallions and garlic until tender; reserve.
2. Wipe down the Instant Pot with a damp cloth. Add Adzuki beans, water, broth, salt, pepper, and paprika.
3. Secure the lid. Choose the "Bean/Chili" mode and High pressure; cook for 20 minutes. Once cooking is complete, use a natural pressure release; carefully remove the lid.
4. Transfer to your food processor and add the reserved scallion/garlic mixture. Then, process the mixture, working in batches. Process until smooth and uniform. Serve warm and enjoy!

Honey Polenta With Toasted Pine Nuts

Serves: 4

Cooking Time: 15 Minutes

Ingredients:

- ½ cup honey
- 5 cups water
- 1 cup polenta
- ½ cup heavy cream
- Salt, to taste
- ¼ cup pine nuts, toasted

Directions:

1. Stir together the honey and water in your Instant Pot.
2. Select the Sauté mode and bring the mixture to a boil, stirring occasionally.
3. Stir in the polenta and lock the lid. Select the Manual mode and set the cooking time for 12 minutes at High Pressure.
4. When the timer beeps, do a quick pressure release. Carefully open the lid.
5. Fold in the heavy creamy and stir until well incorporated. Allow the dish to rest for 1 minute.
6. Season with salt and give it a good stir. Serve topped with toasted pine nuts.

Instant Pot Coconut Oatmeal

Serves: 2

Cooking Time: 3 Minutes

Ingredients:

- 1 cup steel-cut oats
- 2 cups water
- 1 cup coconut milk
- ½ cup coconut sugar
- 1 apple, cored and sliced

Directions:

1. Place all ingredients in the Instant Pot.
2. Stir to combine.
3. Close the lid and press the Manual button.4. Adjust the cooking time to 3 minutes.
4. Do natural pressure release.

Mixed Rice Meal

Serves: 4

Cooking Time: 20 Minutes

Ingredients:

- 3 cups mixture of brown rice and white rice
- 1½ tsps. salt
- 4½ cups water
- 2 tbsps. olive oil

Directions:

1. Add all the ingredients to the pot.
2. Lock the lid. Select the Multigrain mode, then set the timer for 20 minutes at Low Pressure.
3. Once the timer goes off, do a natural pressure release for 10 minutes, then release any remaining pressure. Carefully open the lid.
4. Check if the grains are soft and cooked well. If not, cook for 5 minutes more.
5. Fluff the mixture with a fork and serve.

Speedy Morning Oatmeal

Servings: 4

Cooking Time: 15 Minutes

Ingredients:

- 1 tbsp butter
- 1 tbsp flaxseed
- 3 cups rolled oats
- 1 chocolate square, grated

Directions:

1. Combine butter, oats, flaxseed, and 6 cups of water in your Instant Pot; mix well. Seal the lid, select Pressure Cook, and set the time to 4 minutes. When done, do a quick release. Serve in bowls topped with chocolate.

Black Currant-coconut Rye Porridge

Servings: 2

Cooking Time: 20 Minutes

Ingredients:

- 1 cup rye flakes
- A pinch of salt
- 1 ¼ cups coconut milk
- 1 tsp vanilla extract
- 2 tbsp maple syrup
- ¾ cup frozen black currants

Directions:

1. In your Instant Pot, combine rye flakes, salt, coconut milk, water, vanilla, and maple syrup. Seal the lid, select Pressure Cook on High, and set the time to 5 minutes. After cooking, perform a natural pressure release for 10 minutes. Stir and spoon porridge into serving bowls. Top with black currants and serve warm.

Lentil Chili

Serves: 6-8

Cooking Time: 40 Minutes

Ingredients:

- 1 tbsp olive oil
- 1 onion, diced
- 28 oz canned diced tomatoes, undrained
- 2 cups lentils
- 6 cups vegetable broth

Directions:

1. Select the SAUTÉ setting on the Instant Pot and heat the oil.
2. Add the onion and sauté for about 5 minutes, until softened.
3. Add the tomatoes and sauté for 1 minute more.
4. Add the lentils and broth and stir.
5. Close and lock the lid. Select MANUAL and cook at HIGH pressure for 18 minutes.
6. Once cooking is complete, let the pressure Release Naturally for 15 minutes. Release any remaining steam manually.
7. Open the lid and gently stir. Serve.

Cinnamon Almond Oatmeal

Servings:x

Cooking Time: 15 Minutes | Servings 4

Ingredients:

- 1 ½ cups regular oats
- 2 cups water
- 2 cups almond milk
- 1 teaspoon cinnamon, ground
- 2 tablespoons almond butter
- 1/2 cup chocolate chips

Directions:

1. Simply throw the oats, water, milk, and cinnamon into the Instant Pot.
2. Secure the lid. Choose the "Manual" mode and High pressure; cook for 10 minutes. Once cooking is complete, use a quick pressure release; carefully remove the lid.
3. Divide the oatmeal between serving bowls; top with almond butter and chocolate chips. Enjoy!

Korean Sorghum Pudding

Servings:x

Cooking Time: 25 Minutes

Ingredients:

- 3/4 cup dried sorghum
- 2 cups soy milk
- 1 tablespoon ghee
- 1/3 cup brown sugar
- 1/4 cup cashews, roughly chopped

Directions:

1. Place the dries sorghum, milk, ghee, and brown sugar in the inner pot.
2. Secure the lid. Choose the "Porridge" mode and cook for 20 minutes at High pressure. Once cooking is complete, use a quick pressure release; carefully remove the lid.
3. Serve in individual bowls garnished with chopped cashews. Enjoy!

Bresaola & Black Eyed Peas

Serves: 4

Cooking Time: 35 Minutes

Ingredients:

- ½ lb dried black-eyed peas
- 3 ½ cups chicken stock
- 3 oz bresaola, torn into pieces
- Salt and black pepper to taste

Directions:

1. Place the black-eyed peas and chicken stock in your Instant Pot. Seal the lid, select Manual, and cook for 30 minutes on High pressure. Once ready, allow a natural release for 20 minutes and unlock the lid. Sprinkle with salt and pepper to taste. Serve topped with bresaola.

Pakistani Jeera Rice

Servings:x

Cooking Time: 30 Minutes

Ingredients:

- 3/4 cup rice basmati rice, rinsed
- 1/2 cup water
- 1 cup cream of celery soup
- 1/2 green chili deveined and chopped
- Sea salt and ground black pepper, to taste
- 1 bay leaf
- 1/2 teaspoon Jeera (cumin seeds)
- 1 tablespoon sesame oil

Directions:

1. Place all ingredients in the inner pot. Stir until everything is well combined.
2. Secure the lid. Choose the "Rice" mode and cook for 10 minutes at Low pressure. Once cooking is complete, use a natural pressure

release for 15 minutes; carefully remove the lid.
3. Serve with Indian main dishes of choice. Enjoy!

Authentic Sushi Rice

Servings:x

Cooking Time: 30 Minutes

Ingredients:

- 1 cup sushi rice, rinsed
- 1 cup water
- 2 tablespoons rice vinegar
- 1/2 tablespoon brown sugar
- 1/2 teaspoon salt
- 1 tablespoon soy sauce

Directions:

1. Place the sushi rice and water in the inner pot of your Instant Pot.
2. Secure the lid. Choose the "Rice" mode and cook for 10 minutes at Low pressure. Once cooking is complete, use a natural pressure release for 15 minutes; carefully remove the lid.
3. Meanwhile, whisk the rice vinegar, sugar, salt and soy sauce in a mixing dish; microwave the sauce for 1 minute.
4. Pour the sauce over the sushi rice; stir to combine. Assemble your sushi rolls and enjoy!

Multigrain Rice

Serves: 6 To 8

Cooking Time: 20 Minutes

Ingredients:

- 2 tbsps. olive oil
- 3¾ cups water
- 3 cups wild brown rice
- Salt, to taste

Directions:

1. Combine the oil, water, and brown rice in the pot.
2. Season with salt.
3. Lock the lid. Select the Multigrain mode, then set the timer for 20 minutes on Low Pressure.
4. Once the timer goes off, do a natural pressure release for 5 minutes. Carefully open the lid.
5. Fluff the rice with a fork.
6. Serve immediately.

Raisin Butter Rice

Serves: 4

Cooking Time: 12 Minutes

Ingredients:

- 3 cups wild rice, soaked in water overnight and drained
- 3 cups water
- ½ cup raisins
- ¼ cup salted butter
- 1 tsp. salt

Directions:

1. Add all the ingredients to the Instant Pot.
2. Lock the lid. Select the Rice mode, then set the timer for 12 minutes at Low Pressure.

3. Once the timer goes off, perform a natural release for 8 to 10 minutes.
4. Carefully open the lid and use a fork to fluff the rice.
5. Serve warm.

Brothy Beans With Cream

Serves: 4

Cooking Time: 50 Minutes

Ingredients:

- 2 cups mixed dried heirloom beans, soaked overnight
- 2 quarts chicken stock
- 4 sprigs thyme
- Salt and pepper to taste
- ½ cup heavy cream

Directions:

1. Place all ingredients in the Instant Pot except for the cream.
2. Close the lid and press the Manual button.
3. Adjust the cooking time to 45 minutes.
4. Do quick pressure release.
5. Without the lid on, press the Sauté button and add in the heavy cream.
6. Allow to simmer for 5 minutes.

Cornmeal Porridge

Serves: 2-4

Cooking Time: 20 Minutes

Ingredients:

- 4 cups water
- 1 cup cornmeal
- 1 cup milk
- ½ tsp nutmeg, ground
- ½ cup sweetened condensed milk

Directions:

1. In a bowl, mix 1 cup of water with cornmeal and stir well.
2. Add the rest of the water with milk and cornmeal mix to the Instant Pot and stir.
3. Add nutmeg and stir.
4. Close and secure the lid. Select the MANUAL setting and set the cooking time for 6 minutes at HIGH pressure.
5. Once cooking is complete, use a Natural Release for 10 minutes, then release any remaining pressure.
6. Open the lid. Add condensed milk and stir. Serve.

Mexican Rice

Serves: 4

Cooking Time: 10 Minutes

Ingredients:

- 2 cups long-grain rice
- 2½ cup water
- ½ cup green salsa
- 1 cup cilantro
- 1 avocado
- Salt and pepper, to taste

Directions:

1. Add the rice and water to the Instant Pot.
2. Lock the lid. Select the Rice mode, then set the timer for 5 minutes at Low Pressure.
3. Once the timer goes off, do a natural pressure release for 3 to 5 minutes. Carefully open the lid.
4. Fluff rice and let it cool. Put the salsa, cilantro, and avocado in a blender.
5. Pulse the ingredients together until they are creamy and mix into the rice.
6. Mix everything together and season with salt and pepper.
7. Serve immediately.

Basic Tomato Rice

Serves: 4

Cooking Time:5 Minutes

Ingredients:

- 1 tbsp. extra virgin olive oil
- 2 cups white rice, rinsed and drained
- 4½ cups water
- 1 large, ripe tomato
- Salt and pepper, to taste

Directions:

1. Add olive oil, rice, and water to Instant Pot. Gently stir.
2. Place whole tomato, bottom-side up, in the middle.
3. Lock the lid. Select the Rice mode, then set the timer for 5 minutes at Low Pressure.
4. Once the timer goes off, do a natural pressure release for 3 to 5 minutes, then release any remaining pressure. Carefully open the lid.
5. Using a rice paddle, break up tomato while fluffing up rice. Season with salt and pepper.
6. Serve immediately.

Walnut & Banana Oat Cups

Servings: 2

Cooking Time: 25 Minutes

Ingredients:

- ½ cup steel-cut oats
- 1 banana, mashed
- 1 tsp sugar
- 1 tbsp walnuts, chopped

Directions:

1. Spread the banana onto the bottom of the inner pot. Pour 1 ½ cups water, steel-cut oats, and sugar over the banana. Seal the lid, select Pressure Cook, and cook for 6 minutes on High. When done, do a natural pressure release for 10 minutes, then a quick release. Unlock the lid and stir the oatmeal. Divide between cups. Top with walnuts and serve.

Black Eyed Peas And Ham

Serves: 4-6

Cooking Time: 55 Minutes

Ingredients:

- ½ lb dried black-eyed peas
- 3 ½ cups chicken stock
- 3 oz ham, diced
- Salt and ground black pepper to taste

Directions:

1. Add the peas, chicken stock and ham to the Instant Pot.
2. Close and secure the lid. Select MANUAL and cook at HIGH pressure for 30 minutes.
3. Once cooking is complete, select CANCEL and let Naturally Release for 20 minutes. Open the lid.
4. Add salt and pepper to taste if needed. Serve.

Fish & Seafood Recipes

Fish & Seafood Recipes

Salmon Fillets

Serves: 3

Cooking Time: 03 Minutes

Ingredients:

- 1 cup water
- 3 lemon slices
- 1 5-oz.) salmon fillet
- 1 teaspoon fresh lemon juice
- Salt and ground black pepper, to taste
- Fresh cilantro to garnish

Directions:

1. Add the water to the Instant pot and place a trivet inside.
2. In a shallow bowl, place the salmon fillet. Sprinkle salt and pepper over it.
3. Squeeze some lemon juice on top then place a lemon slice over the salmon fillet.
4. Cover the lid and lock it. Set its pressure release handle to "Sealing" position.
5. Use "Steam" function on your cooker for 3 minutes to cook.
6. After the beep, do a Quick release and release the steam.
7. Remove the lid, then serve with the lemon slice and fresh cilantro on top.

Cod Platter

Serves: 6

Cooking Time: 05 Minutes

Ingredients:

- 1 ½ lbs. cherry tomatoes, halved
- 2 ½ tablespoons fresh rosemary, chopped
- 6 4-oz.) cod fillets
- 3 garlic cloves, minced
- 2 tablespoons olive oil
- Salt and freshly ground black pepper, to taste

Directions:

1. Add the olive oil, half of the tomatoes and rosemary to the insert of the Instant Pot.
2. Place the cod fillets over these tomatoes. Then add more tomatoes to the pot.
3. Add the garlic to the pot. Then secure the lid.
4. Select the "Manual" function with high pressure for 5 minutes.
5. After the beep, use the quick release to discharge all the steam.
6. Serve cod fillets with tomatoes and sprinkle a pinch of salt and pepper on top.

Steamed Herbed Red Snapper

Serves: 4

Cooking Time: 12 Minutes

Ingredients:

- 1 cup water
- 4 red snapper fillets
- 1½ tsps. chopped fresh herbs
- ¼ tsp. paprika
- 3 tbsps. freshly squeezed lemon juice
- Salt and pepper, to taste

Directions:

1. Set a trivet in the Instant Pot and pour the water into the pot.
2. Mix all ingredients in a heat-proof dish that will fit in the Instant Pot. Combine to coat the fish with all ingredients.
3. Place the heat-proof dish on the trivet.
4. Lock the lid. Select the Manual mode and cook for 12 minutes at Low Pressure.
5. Once cooking is complete, do a quick pressure release. Carefully open the lid.
6. Serve warm.

Old Bay Fish Tacos

Serves: 4

Cooking Time: 8 Minutes

Ingredients:

- 2 large cod fillets
- 1 tablespoon old bay seasoning
- 1/2 cup quesadilla cheese

Directions:

1. Place a trivet or a steamer basket in the Instant Pot. Pour a cup of water.
2. Season the cod fillets with old bay seasoning.

3. Place on top of the steamer rack.
4. Close the lid and press the Steam button.
5. Adjust the cooking time to 10 minutes.
6. Do quick pressure release.
7. Serve with quesadilla cheese on top.

Mussels With White Wine

Serves: 4

Cooking Time: 15 Minutes

Ingredients:

- 3 lbs mussels, cleaned and debearded
- 6 tbsp butter
- 4 shallots, chopped
- 1 cup white wine
- 1½ cups chicken stock

Directions:

1. Add the butter to the Instant Pot and select SAUTÉ.
2. Once the butter has melted, add the shallots and sauté for 2 minutes.
3. Pour in the wine, stir and cook for another 1 minute.
4. Add the stock and mussels, stir well. Close and lock the lid.
5. Press the CANCEL button to stop the SAUTE function, then select the MANUAL setting and set the cooking time for 3 minutes at HIGH pressure.
6. Once pressure cooking is complete, use a Quick Release. Unlock and carefully open the lid.
7. Remove unopened mussels and serve.

Delicious And Simple Octopus

Serves: 4

Cooking Time: 15 Minutes

Ingredients:

- ¼ tsp. sweet paprika
- 2 lbs. octopus, rinsed
- Salt and black pepper, to taste
- ¼ tsp. chili powder

Directions:

1. Season octopus with salt and pepper, add to the Instant Pot.
2. Add enough water to cover, then add chili powder and paprika, stir a bit.
3. Lock the lid. Select the Manual mode and cook for 15 minutes at Low Pressure.
4. Once cooking is complete, do a quick pressure release. Carefully open the lid.
5. Cut the octopus and serve.

Easy Lobster Tails With Butter

Serves: 4

Cooking Time: 10 Minutes

Ingredients:

- 1 ½ pounds lobster tails, halved
- 1/2 stick butter, at room temperature
- Sea salt and freshly ground black pepper, to taste
- 1/2 teaspoon red pepper flakes

Directions:

1. Add a metal trivet, steamer basket, and 1 cup of water in your Instant Pot.
2. Place the lobster tails, shell side down, in the prepared steamer basket.
3. Secure the lid. Choose the "Steam" mode and cook for 3 minutes at Low pressure.

Once cooking is complete, use a quick pressure release; carefully remove the lid.

4. Drizzle with butter. Season with salt, black pepper, and red pepper and serve immediately. Enjoy!

Sole Fillets With Pickle Mayo

Servings:x

Cooking Time: 10 Minutes | Servings 4

Ingredients:

- 1 ½ pounds sole fillets
- Sea salt and ground black pepper, to taste
- 1 teaspoon paprika
- 1/2 cup mayonnaise
- 1 tablespoon pickle juice
- 2 cloves garlic, smashed

Directions:

1. Sprinkle the fillets with salt, black pepper, and paprika.
2. Add 1 ½ cups of water and a steamer basket to the Instant Pot. Place the fish in the steamer basket.
3. Secure the lid and choose "Manual" setting. Cook for 3 minutes at Low pressure. Once cooking is complete, use a quick release; carefully remove the lid.
4. Then, make the sauce by mixing the mayonnaise with pickle juice and garlic. Serve the fish fillets with the well-chilled sauce on the side. Bon appétit!

Shrimp Green Curry

Serves: 5

Cooking Time: 60 Minutes

Ingredients:

- 7 oz. cleaned and deveined shrimps
- 4 tbsps. Thai basil leaves
- 2 tbsps. green curry paste
- 1 tsp. coconut oil
- 4 tsps. fish sauce

Directions:

1. Press the Sauté bottom on the Instant Pot.
2. Add and heat the oil in the Instant Pot.
3. Add the chili and shrimp; sauté for 2 minutes.
4. Add the fish sauce, paste, and basil; cook for 1 minute more.
5. Lock the lid. Select the Manual mode and cook for 60 minutes at Low Pressure.
6. Once cooking is complete, do a quick pressure release. Carefully open the lid.
7. Transfer the cooked recipe on serving plates.
8. Serve the recipe warm.

Szechuan Shrimps

Serves: 4

Cooking Time: 6 Minutes

Ingredients:

- 1 tbsp. julienned ginger
- 1½ lbs. unpeeled raw shrimps
- 3 tbsps. soy sauce
- 2 tbsps. crushed red pepper
- Salt and pepper, to taste
- 3 tbsps. chopped green scallions

Directions:

1. Place all ingredients in the Instant Pot.

2. Lock the lid. Select the Manual mode and cook for 6 minutes at Low Pressure.
3. Once cooking is complete, do a quick pressure release. Carefully open the lid.
4. Garnish with green scallions and serve.

Mussels With Lemon & White Wine

Serves: 5

Cooking Time: 15 Minutes

Ingredients:

- 1 cup white wine
- ½ cup water
- 1 tsp garlic powder
- 2 pounds mussels, cleaned and debearded
- Juice from 1 lemon

Directions:

1. In the pot, mix garlic powder, water and wine. Put the mussels into the steamer basket, rounded-side should be placed facing upwards to fit as many as possible.
2. Insert rack into the cooker and lower steamer basket onto the rack. Seal the lid and cook on Low Pressure for 1 minute. Release the pressure quickly. Remove unopened mussels. Coat the mussels with the wine mixture and lemon juice to serve.

Fast Shrimp Scampi

Serves: 4

Cooking Time: 4 Minutes

Ingredients:

- 1 cup chicken stock
- 2 tbsps. butter
- Juice of 1 lemon
- 1 lb. shrimp, peeled and deveined
- 2 shallots, chopped

Directions:

1. Set the Instant Pot on Sauté mode, add butter, heat it up.
2. Add shallots and sauté for 1 to 2 minutes.
3. Add shrimp, lemon juice and stock, stir.
4. Lock the lid. Select the Manual mode and cook for 2 minutes at Low Pressure.
5. Once cooking is complete, do a quick pressure release. Carefully open the lid.
6. Divide into bowls and serve.

Dijon Salmon

Serves: 2

Cooking Time: 15 Minutes

Ingredients:

- 2 fish fillets or steaks, such as salmon, cod, or halibut (1-inch thick)
- 1 cup water
- Salt and ground black pepper to taste
- 2 tsp Dijon mustard

Directions:

1. Pour the water into the Instant Pot and insert a steam rack.
2. Sprinkle the fish with salt and pepper.
3. Place the fillets on the rack skin-side down and spread the Dijon mustard on top of each fillets or steaks.
4. Close and lock the lid. Select MANUAL and cook at HIGH pressure for 5 minutes.
5. When the timer goes off, use a Quick Release. Carefully open the lid.

Alfredo Tuscan Shrimp

Serves: 3

Cooking Time: 15 Minutes

Ingredients:

- 1 lb. shrimp
- 1 jar alfredo sauce
- 1 ½ cups fresh spinach
- 1 cup sun-dried tomatoes
- 1 box penne pasta1 ½ teaspoon Tuscan seasoning3 cups water

Directions:

1. Add the water and pasta to a pot over a medium heat, boil until it cooks completely. Then strain the pasta and keep it aside.
2. Select the "Sauté" function on your Instant Pot and add the tomatoes, shrimp, Tuscan seasoning, and alfredo sauce into it.
3. Stir and cook until shrimp turn pink in color.
4. Now add the spinach leaves to the pot and cook for 5 minutes.
5. Add the pasta to the pot and stir well.
6. Serve hot.

Salmon, Broccoli And Potatoes

Serves: 2-4

Cooking Time: 30 Minutes

Ingredients:

- 2 salmon fillets
- Salt and ground black pepper to taste
- Fresh herbs, optional
- 1 cup water
- 1 lb new potatoes
- 1 cups broccoli, chopped
- ½ tbsp butter

Directions:

1. In a bowl, season the potatoes with salt, pepper and fresh herbs.
2. Prepare the Instant Pot by adding the water to the pot and placing the steam rack in it.
3. Place the potatoes on the steam rack, close and lock the lid.
4. Select MANUAL and cook at HIGH pressure for 2 minutes.
5. Meanwhile, in a bowl, season the broccoli and salmon with salt and pepper.
6. When the timer goes off, use a quick release. Carefully open the lid.
7. Place the broccoli and salmon on the steam rack, along with the potatoes.
8. Close and lock the lid. Select MANUAL and cook at HIGH pressure for 2 minutes more.
9. When the timer beeps, use a Natural Release for 10 minutes. Uncover the pot.
10. Transfer the potatoes to a separate bowl and add the butter. Gently stir to coat the potatoes with the butter.
11. Serve the cooked fish with potatoes and broccoli.

Oysters-in-the-shell

Serves: 6

Cooking Time: 15 Minutes

Ingredients:

- 36 in-shell oysters
- 1 cup water
- Salt and ground black pepper to taste
- 6 tbsp butter, melted

Directions:

1. Clean the oysters well.
2. Add the water, oysters, salt and pepper to the Instant Pot
3. Close and lock the lid. Select the MANUAL setting and set the cooking time for 3 minutes at HIGH pressure.
4. When the timer beeps, use a Quick Release. Carefully unlock the lid.
5. Serve with melted butter.

Cod Meal

Serves: 2

Cooking Time: 5 Minutes

Ingredients:

- 1 cup water
- 2 tbsps. ghee
- 1 fresh large fillet cod
- Salt and pepper, to taste

Directions:

1. Cut fillet into 3 pieces. Coat with the ghee and season with salt and pepper.
2. Pour the water into the pot and place steamer basket/trivet inside.
3. Arrange the fish pieces over the basket/trivet.
4. Lock the lid. Select the Manual mode and cook for 5 minutes at Low Pressure.
5. Once cooking is complete, do a quick pressure release. Carefully open the lid.
6. Serve warm.

Mediterranean Cod With Capers

Serves: 4

Cooking Time: 15 Minutes

Ingredients:

- 4 cod fillets, boneless
- ½ cup white wine
- 1 tsp oregano
- Salt and black pepper to taste.
- ¼ cup capers

Directions:

1. Pour the white wine and ½ cup of water in your Instant Pot and fit in a trivet. Place cod fillets on the trivet and sprinkle with oregano, salt, and pepper. Seal the lid, select Steam, and cook for 3 minutes on Low. Once ready, perform a quick pressure release and unlock the lid. Top the cod with capers and drizzle with the sauce to serve.

Simple Shrimp

Serves: 3

Cooking Time: 3 Minutes

Ingredients:

- ½ cup chicken stock
- ½ cup white wine
- 2 tbsps. olive oil
- 1 tbsp. minced garlic
- 2 lbs. shrimp, deveined and peeled

Directions:

1. Set the Instant Pot on Sauté mode, add oil, heat it up.
2. Add garlic and sauté for 30 seconds.
3. Add shrimp, wine and stock, stir.
4. Lock the lid. Select the Manual mode and cook for 3 minutes at Low Pressure.
5. Once cooking is complete, do a quick pressure release. Carefully open the lid.
6. Divide into bowls and serve.

Lemon Tuna Steaks With Capers

Servings: 2

Cooking Time: 15 Minutes

Ingredients:

- 4 tbsp olive oil
- 2 tuna steaks
- Salt and black pepper to taste
- 1 lemon, zested and juiced
- 2 tbsp chopped thyme
- 3 tbsp drained capers

Directions:

1. Pour 1 cup of water into your Instant Pot and fit in a trivet. Drizzle tuna with some olive oil and season with salt and pepper. Place it on the trivet. Seal the lid, select Pressure Cook, and set the time to 6 minutes. After cooking, do a quick release. Remove fish to a serving plate. Empty and clean inner pot. Set to Sauté and heat the remaining olive oil. Sauté lemon zest and juice, capers, and 2 tbsp of water for 3 minutes. Pour sauce over tuna and garnish with thyme.

Vegetable & Vegetarian Recipes

Vegetable & Vegetarian Recipes

Maple Glazed Carrots

Serves: 4-6

Cooking Time: 40 Minutes

Ingredients:

- 2/3 cup water
- 2 lbs carrots, sliced into ½ inch diagonal pieces
- ¼ cup raisins
- 1 tbsp maple syrup
- 1 tbsp butter
- Salt and ground black pepper to taste

Directions:

1. Add the water, carrots and raisins to the Instant Pot.
2. Secure the lid. Select the MANUAL setting and set the cooking time for 4 minutes at HIGH pressure.
3. Once pressure cooking is complete, select CANCEL and use a Quick Release. Carefully unlock the lid.
4. Transfer the carrots to a bowl.
5. Carefully pour the water out of the pot and completely dry the pot before replacing it.
6. Select SAUTÉ; add the butter and maple syrup.
7. Return the carrots to the pot and stir well until fully coated with butter.
8. Press the CANCEL key to stop the SAUTÉ function.
9. Season with salt and pepper. Serve.

Corn And Potato Chowder

Servings:6

Cooking Time: 40 Minutes

Ingredients:

- 4 russet potatoes, peeled and cubed
- Kernels from 2 ears corn
- 2 teaspoons dried thyme
- 2 teaspoons freshly ground black pepper
- 2 teaspoons kosher salt
- 1 teaspoon onion powder
- 3½ cups water

Directions:

1. In the inner pot, combine the potatoes, corn, thyme, pepper, salt, onion powder, and water.
2. Lock the lid into place. Select Pressure Cook or Manual; set the pressure to High and the time to 12 minutes.
3. After the cook time is complete, let the pressure release Naturally. Unlock and remove the lid.
4. Using an immersion blender, puree the soup. Stir and adjust the seasoning. Serve hot.

Mediterranean Green Beans With Nuts

Servings: 4

Cooking Time: 15 Minutes

Ingredients:

- 2 tbsp olive oil
- 1 lb green beans, trimmed
- 1 lemon, juiced
- 2 tbsp toasted peanuts, chopped

Directions:

1. Pour 1 cup of water, fit in a steamer basket, and arrange green beans on top. Seal the lid, select Pressure Cook on High, and set the time to 1 minute. After cooking, do a quick pressure release to let out steam, and unlock the lid. Remove green beans onto a plate and mix in lemon juice, olive oil, and peanuts. Serve immediately.

Mixed Vegetables Medley

Serves: 4

Cooking Time: 15 Minutes

Ingredients:

- 1 small head broccoli, broken into florets
- 16 asparagus, trimmed
- 1 small head cauliflower, broken into florets
- 5 ounces green beans
- 2 carrots, peeled and cut on bias
- Salt to taste

Directions:

1. Add 1 cup of water and set trivet on top of water and place steamer basket on top. In an even layer, spread green beans, broccoli, cauliflower, asparagus, and carrots in the steamer basket. Seal the lid and cook on

Steam for 3 minutes on High. Release the pressure quickly. Remove basket from the pot and season with salt.

Baked Potatoes

Serves: 8

Cooking Time: 30 Minutes

Ingredients:

- 5 lbs potatoes, peeled and cut into half
- 1½ cups water
- Salt to taste

Directions:

1. Prepare the Instant Pot by adding the water to the pot and placing the steamer basket in it.
2. Place the potatoes in the basket. Close and secure the lid.
3. Select the MANUAL setting and set the cooking time for 10 minutes at HIGH pressure.
4. Once cooking is complete, let the pressure Release Naturally for 15 minutes. Release any remaining steam manually. Uncover the pot.
5. Season with salt and serve.

Steamed Sweet Potatoes With Cilantro

Serves: 4

Cooking Time: 20 Minutes

Ingredients:

- 2 tbsp butter, melted
- 1 lb sweet potatoes, scrubbed
- 2 tbsp fresh cilantro, chopped

Directions:

1. Pour 1 cup of water in your Instant Pot and fit in a trivet. Place the potatoes on the trivet. Seal the lid, select Manual, and cook for 12 minutes on High pressure. When done, perform a quick pressure release and unlock the lid. Drizzle with melted butter and sprinkle with cilantro to serve.

Squash Porridge

Serves: 2-4

Cooking Time: 20 Minutes

Ingredients:

- 1 squash, peeled and chopped
- 3 apples, cored and chopped
- 2 tbsp cinnamon powder
- 2 tbsp maple syrup
- ¾ cup water
- Salt to taste

Directions:

1. Combine all of the ingredients in the Instant Pot and stir to mix.
2. Close and lock the lid. Select the MANUAL setting and set the cooking time for 8 minutes at HIGH pressure.
3. Once pressure cooking is complete, select CANCEL and use a Quick Release. Careful-

ly unlock the lid.
4. Stir the porridge and serve.

Steamed Artichokes With Salsa Roquefort

Serves: 2-4

Cooking Time: 20 Minutes

Ingredients:

- 1 lb artichokes, trimmed
- 1 lemon wedge
- ½ cup roquefort cheese
- 1 cup heavy cream

Directions:

1. Pour 1 cup of water in your Instant Pot and fit in a steamer basket. Place in artichokes and seal the lid. Select Manual and cook for 10 minutes on High pressure.
2. When over, perform a quick pressure release, and unlock the lid. Remove artichokes to a plate to cool. Clean the pot and heat the heavy cream on Sauté. Add in the roquefort cheese and stir constantly until the cheese melts, about 3-4 minutes.Pour the sauce over the artichokes and serve.

Pumpkin Stew

Serves: 4

Cooking Time: 25 Minutes

Ingredients:

- 3 cups pumpkin, peeled and cubed (1 inch thick)
- 1 large can diced tomatoes
- 5 cups vegetable stock
- 3 cups mixed greens
- Salt and ground black pepper to taste

Directions:

1. Combine all of the ingredients in the Instant Pot and stir to mix.
2. Close and lock the lid. Select MANUAL and cook at HIGH pressure for 10 minutes.
3. When the timer beeps, use a Quick Release. Carefully unlock the lid.
4. Taste for seasoning and add more salt if needed. Serve.

Spicy Mozzarella Omelet Cups

Serves: 2

Cooking Time 20 Minutes

Ingredients:

- ¼ cup shredded mozzarella cheese
- 1 tsp olive oil
- 4 eggs, beaten
- Salt and black pepper to taste
- 1 onion, chopped
- 1 spicy chili pepper, chopped

Directions:

1. Grease two ramekins with olive oil. Beat eggs, water, salt, and black pepper in a bowl. Mix in onion and chili pepper.Divide the mixture into the ramekins and top with mozzarella cheese. Pour 1 cup of water in your Instant Pot and fit in a trivet. Place the ramekins on top of the trivet and seal the lid. Select Manual and cook for 15 minutes on High pressure. When ready, perform a quick pressure release and unlock the lid. Serve immediately.

Prosciutto Wrapped Asparagus

Serves: 2-4

Cooking Time: 15 Minutes

Ingredients:

- 1½ cups water
- 1 lb asparagus
- 10 oz prosciutto, sliced

Directions:

1. Wash asparagus and trim off bottom of stems by about 1 inch.
2. Prepare the Instant Pot by adding the water to the pot and placing the steam rack in it.
3. Wrap the prosciutto slices around the asparagus spears.
4. Place the un-wrapped asparagus on the rack, and then place the prosciutto-wrapped spears on top.
5. Close and lock the lid. Select MANUAL and cook at HIGH pressure for 3 minutes.
6. When the timer goes off, let the pressure Release Naturally for 5 minutes, then release any remaining steam manually. Open the lid.
7. Serve.

Cauliflower Patties

Serves: 4

Cooking Time: 30 Minutes

Ingredients:

- 1½ cups water
- 1 cauliflower head, chopped
- 1 cup ground almonds
- 1 cup vegan cheese, shredded
- Salt and ground black pepper to taste
- 2 tbsp olive oil

Directions:

1. Pour the water into the Instant Pot and insert a steamer basket.
2. Put the cauliflower in to the basket.
3. Close and lock the lid. Select MANUAL and cook at HIGH pressure for 5 minutes.
4. Once timer goes off, use a Quick Release. Carefully unlock the lid.
5. Place the cauliflower in a food processor and ground it.
6. Add the almonds and cheese. Season with salt and pepper. Mix well.
7. Shape the mixture into oval patties each ½ inch thick.
8. Carefully pour the water out of the pot and completely dry the pot before replacing it.
9. Select the SAUTÉ setting on the Instant Pot and heat the oil.
10. Add the patties and cook on both sides until golden. You may have to do it in two batches.
11. Serve.

Cauliflower Pasta

Serves: 6

Cooking Time: 20 Minutes

Ingredients:

- 1 cup chopped cauliflower
- 2 tbsps. chopped green onions
- 12 oz. vermicelli pasta
- 1 tsp. olive oil
- 1 small green chili pepper, chopped

Directions:

1. In the Instant Pot; add the pasta and enough water to cover.
2. Lock the lid. Set the Instant Pot to Manual mode, then set the timer for 7 minutes at High Pressure.
3. Once cooking is complete, do a quick pressure release. Carefully open the lid.
4. Drain water and transfer the cooked pasta in a container.
5. Take the Instant Pot and place over dry kitchen surface; open its top lid and switch it on.
6. Press Sauté. Grease the pot with olive oil.
7. Add the cauliflower; cook for 7 to 8 minutes until turn softened.
8. Mix in the pasta and serve warm. Top with the green onions.

Steamed Lemon Artichokes

Serves: 4

Cooking Time: 20 Minutes

Ingredients:

- 1 cup water
- 2 garlic cloves, minced
- Salt, to taste
- 1 bay leaf
- 4 artichokes, trimmed
- 2 tbsps. freshly squeezed lemon juice

Directions:

1. Mix the water, garlic, salt and bay leaf inside the Instant Pot.
2. Place steamer basket in the pot.
3. Add the artichokes.
4. Drizzle each one with lemon juice.
5. Lock the lid. Set the Instant Pot to Steam mode, then set the timer for 10 minutes at High Pressure.
6. Once cooking is complete, do a quick pressure release. Carefully open the lid.
7. Remove outer petals and discard.
8. Discard the bay leaf, slice the artichokes into pieces and serve.

Pure Basmati Rice Meal

Serves: 4

Cooking Time: 10 Minutes

Ingredients:

- 1 cup chopped cauliflower
- ¼ cup chopped green onions
- 1 small onion, sliced
- 1 cup basmati rice
- 1 tsp. olive oil

Directions:

1. Purée the cauliflower until smooth in a blender and set aside.
2. Press the Sauté bottom on the Instant Pot. Grease the pot with olive oil.
3. Add the onions and sauté for 3 minutes until translucent and softened.
4. Add the cauliflower purée, rice and green onions.
5. Lock the lid. Set the Instant Pot to Manual mode, then set the timer for 4 minutes at Low Pressure.
6. Once cooking is complete, do a natural pressure release. Carefully open the lid.
7. Transfer the cooked recipe on serving plates.
8. Serve warm.

Crushed Potatoes With Aioli

Serves: 4

Cooking Time: 25 Minutes

Ingredients:

- 1 lb Russet potatoes, pierced
- Salt and black pepper to taste
- 2 tbsp olive oil
- 4 tbsp mayonnaise
- 1 tsp garlic paste
- 1 tbsp lemon juice

Directions:

1. Mix olive oil, salt, and pepper in a bowl. Add in the potatoes and toss to coat. Pour 1 cup of water in your Instant Pot and fit in a trivet. Place the potatoes on the trivet and seal the lid. Select Manual and cook for 12 minutes on High.
2. Once ready, perform a quick pressure release and unlock the lid. In a small bowl, combine mayonnaise, garlic paste, and lemon juice; mix well. Peel and crush the potatoes and transfer to a serving bowl. Serve with aioli.

Caramelized Onions

Serves: 2

Cooking Time: 35 Minutes

Ingredients:

- 1 tbsp. freshly squeezed lemon juice
- 3 tbsps. coconut oil
- Salt and pepper, to taste
- 3 white onions, sliced
- 1 cup water

Directions:

1. Press the Sauté button on the Instant Pot and heat the coconut oil.
2. Sauté the onions for 5 minutes and add the remaining ingredients.
3. Add the water and stir.
4. Lock the lid. Set the Instant Pot to Manual mode, then set the timer for 20 minutes at High Pressure.
5. Once cooking is complete, do a quick pressure release. Carefully open the lid.
6. Press the Sauté button and continue cooking for another 10 minutes.
7. Serve warm.

Mango Tofu Curry

Serves: 2

Cooking Time: 35 Minutes

Ingredients:

- 1 cup vegetable broth
- 1lb. vegetables, chopped
- 2 tbsps. curry paste
- 1lb. cubed extra firm tofu
- 1 cup mango sauce
- Salt and pepper, to taste

Directions:

1. Mix all the ingredients in the Instant Pot.
2. Lock the lid. Set the Instant Pot to Manual mode, then set the timer for 35 minutes at High Pressure.
3. Once cooking is complete, do a quick pressure release. Carefully open the lid.
4. Serve warm.

Instant Pot Mushrooms

Serves: 1

Cooking Time: 10 Minutes

Ingredients:

- ½ cup water
- 4 oz. mushrooms, sliced
- 2 garlic cloves, minced
- 1 tbsp. olive oil
- Salt and pepper, to taste

Directions:

1. Pour water along with mushrooms in an Instant Pot.
2. Lock the lid. Set the Instant Pot to Manual mode, then set the timer for 5 minutes at High Pressure.
3. Once cooking is complete, do a quick pressure release. Carefully open the lid.
4. Drain the mushroom and then return back to the Instant Pot.
5. Now add olive oil to the pot and mix.
6. Press the Sauté function of the pot and let it cook for 3 minutes.
7. Sauté every 30 seconds.
8. Add the garlic and sauté for 2 minutes or until fragrant. Sprinkle with salt and pepper, then serve the dish.

Soups, Stews & Chilis Recipes

Soups, Stews & Chilis Recipes

Black Chicken Stew

Serves:4

Cooking Time: 30 Minutes

Ingredients:

- 2 tbsp mixed berries
- 3 slices of fresh ginger
- A handful of walnuts
- A handful of dates
- Salt and black pepper to taste
- 1 (3.5-oz) whole black chicken

Directions:

1. Clean the insides of the chicken. Add ½ cup water to your IP. In a mixing bowl, mix all the ingredients together with your hands. Stuff the mixture into the chicken and place in the cooker. Season with salt and pepper. Seal the lid, select Manual at High, and cook for 20 minutes. When ready, release the pressure naturally for 5 minutes. Remove the chicken from the pot. Slice and place on Serves: plates.

Potato Soup

Serves: 8

Cooking Time: 15 Minutes

Ingredients:

- 3 lbs. potatoes, peeled and cubed
- 2 cups milk
- ¼ tsp. salt
- 12 green onions, chopped
- 1 cup shredded Cheddar cheese

Directions:

1. In the Instant Pot, mix the potatoes with milk and salt. Stir to combine.
2. Lock the lid. Select the Manual mode and set the timer for 12 minutes at High Pressure.
3. Once the timer goes off, do a quick pressure release. Carefully open the lid.
4. Add the Cheddar cheese and green onions, and stir to mix well.
5. Set the pot to Sauté and cook until the cheese melts, about 3 minutes.
6. Ladle the soup into bowls and serve.

Salmon Meatballs Soup

Serves: 5

Cooking Time: 10 Minutes

Ingredients:

- 2 tbsps. melted butter
- 2 garlic cloves, minced
- 2 large eggs, beaten
- 1 lb. ground salmon
- Salt and pepper, to taste
- 2 cups hot water

Directions:

1. In a bowl, mix the butter, garlic, eggs and salmon. Sprinkle with salt and pepper.
2. Combine the mixture and use the hands to form the mixture into small balls.
3. Place the fish balls in the freezer to set for 2 hours or until frozen.
4. Pour the hot water in the Instant Pot and drop in the frozen fish balls.
5. Lock the lid. Select the Manual mode and set the timer to 10 minutes at Low Pressure.
6. When the timer goes off, perform a quick release.
7. Carefully open the lid. Allow to cool for a few minutes and remove the fish balls from the pot. Serve immediately.

Noodle & Chicken Soup

Serves: 2-4

Cooking Time: 40 Minutes

Ingredients:

- 1 lb chicken breasts, chopped
- ½ cup egg noodles
- 4 cups chicken broth
- A handful of fresh parsley
- 1 tsp salt

- ¼ tsp black pepper

Directions:

1. Season the filets with salt and place in the pot. Pour the broth and seal the lid. Cook on Soup/Broth for 20 minutes on High. Do a quick release. Add in the noodles and seal the lid again.
2. Press the Manual/Pressure Cook and cook for 5 minutes on High Pressure. Release the pressure quickly, and sprinkle with freshly ground black pepper and parsley. Serve warm.

Coconut Celery Soup

Serves: 8

Cooking Time: 30 Minutes

Ingredients:

- 2 bunches celery, diced
- 2 sweet yellow onions, diced
- 2 cups coconut milk4 cups chicken broth
- 1 teaspoon dill
- 2 pinches of sea salt

Directions:

1. Put all the ingredients into the instant pot.
2. Secure the lid and set the cooker on the 'soup' function for 30 minutes.
3. After the beep, use 'natural release' to vent the steam, then remove the lid.
4. Use an immerse blender to blend the soup into a smooth mixture.
5. Serve hot.

Turmeric Chicken Soup

Serves: 3

Cooking Time: 15 Minutes

Ingredients:

- 3 boneless chicken breasts
- 1 bay leaf
- ½ cup coconut milk
- 2½ tsps. turmeric powder
- 4 cups water

Directions:

1. Place all the ingredients in the Instant Pot. Stir to combine well.
2. Lock the lid. Set to Poultry mode and set the timer to 15 minutes at High Pressure.
3. When the timer goes off, perform a natural pressure release for 10 minutes, then release any remaining pressure.
4. Carefully open the lid. Allow to cool for a few minutes, then serve immediately.

Asian Egg Drop Soup

Serves: 3

Cooking Time: 9 Minutes

Ingredients:

- 1 tsp. grated ginger
- 3 cups water
- 2 cups chopped kale
- 3 tbsps. coconut oil
- Salt and pepper, to taste
- 2 eggs, beaten

Directions:

1. Place all ingredients, except for the beaten eggs, in the Instant Pot.
2. Lock the lid. Set the Manual mode and set the timer to 6 minutes at High Pressure.

3. When the timer goes off, perform a natural pressure release for 5 minutes, then release any remaining pressure.
4. Carefully open the lid. Press the Sauté button and bring the soup to a simmer.
5. Gradually pour in the beaten eggs and allow to simmer for 3 more minutes.
6. Pour the soup in a large bowl and serve warm.

Cabbage Soup

Serves: 2

Cooking Time: 35 Minutes

Ingredients:

- 1 onion, shredded
- 1lb. cabbage, shredded
- 1 tbsp. black pepper
- 2 tbsps. mixed herbs
- 1 cup low-sodium vegetable broth

Directions:

1. Mix all the ingredients in the Instant Pot.
2. Lock the lid. Select the Soup mode, then set the timer for 35 minutes at High Pressure.
3. Once the timer goes off, do a quick pressure release. Carefully open the lid.
4. Serve warm.

Chili Con Carne (chili With Meat)

Serves: 2

Cooking Time: 35 Minutes

Ingredients:

- 2 cups chopped tomatoes
- 3 tbsps. mixed seasoning
- 1lb. ground beef
- 3 squares dark chocolate
- 1 cup mixed beans

Directions:

1. Mix all the ingredients in the Instant Pot.
2. Lock the lid. Select the Meat/Stew setting. Set the timer for 35 minutes at High Pressure.
3. Once cooking is complete, perform a natural pressure release for 10 minutes, then release any remaining pressure. Carefully open the lid.
4. Serve warm.

Salmon Head Soup

Serves: 1

Cooking Time: 12 Minutes

Ingredients:

- 1 tsp. coconut oil
- 1 onion, sliced
- 3 cups water
- 1 salmon head
- 3-inch ginger piece, slivered
- Salt and pepper, to taste

Directions:

1. Press the Sauté button on the Instant Pot and heat the coconut oil.
2. Sauté the onion for 3 minutes or until trans-lucent.
3. Pour in the water, then add the salmon head and ginger.
4. Sprinkle salt and pepper for seasoning.
5. Lock the lid. Set on the Manual mode, then set the timer to 10 minutes at Low Pressure.
6. When the timer goes off, perform a quick release.
7. Carefully open the lid. Allow to cool before serving.

Lemon Chicken Soup

Serves: 4

Cooking Time: 8 Minutes

Ingredients:

- 2 tbsps. lemon juice
- 6 cups chicken stock
- 3 chicken breast fillets
- 1 tsp. garlic powder
- 1 diced onion
- Salt and pepper, to taste

Directions:

1. Put the chicken stock, chicken breast fillets, garlic powder, and onion in the Instant Pot and mix well.
2. Lock the lid. Select the Manual mode, then set the timer for 6 minutes at High Pressure.
3. Once the timer goes off, do a natural pressure release for 5 minutes, then release any remaining pressure. Carefully open the lid.
4. Remove the chicken and shred.
5. Put it back to the pot and set the Instant Pot to Sauté.
6. Whisk in the lemon juice. Season with salt and pepper. Serve immediately.

Poached Egg Chicken Bone Soup

Serves: 2

Cooking Time: 36 Minutes

Ingredients:

- 1 lb. chicken bones
- 1 tsp. olive oil
- 2 cups water
- 2 whole eggs
- 1 romaine lettuce head, chopped
- Salt and pepper, to taste

Directions:

1. Place the chicken bones, olive oil, and water in the Instant Pot.
2. Lock the lid. Set to Poultry mode and the timer to 30 minutes at High Pressure.
3. When the timer goes off, do a natural pressure release for 10 minutes, then release any remaining pressure.
4. Carefully open the lid, then discard the bones with tongs.
5. Press the Sauté button and bring the soup to a simmer.
6. Carefully crack the eggs in the pot and simmer for 3 minutes.
7. Add the lettuce and season with salt and pepper.
8. Allow to simmer for 3 more minutes.
9. Serve warm.

Chinese Congee

Serves: 6

Cooking Time: 20minutes

Ingredients:

- 1 lb ground chicken6 cups chicken broth
- ½ tablespoon salt1½ cups short grain rice,

rinsed until water is clear
- 1 tablespoon grated fresh ginger
- 4 cups cabbage, shredded
- Green onions to garnish

Directions:

1. Put all the ingredients, except the cabbage and green onions, in the instant pot.
2. Select the 'porridge' function and cook on the default time and settings.
3. After the beep, 'quick release' the steam and remove the lid.
4. Stir in the shredded cabbage and cover with the lid.
5. Serve after 10 minutes with chopped green onions on top.

Fish Soup

Serves: 4

Cooking Time: 8 Minutes

Ingredients:

- 1 lb. boneless, skinless and cubed white fish fillets
- 1 carrot, chopped
- 1 cup chopped bacon
- 4 cups chicken stock
- Salt and pepper, to taste
- 2 cups heavy whipping cream

Directions:

1. In the Instant Pot, mix the fish with carrot, bacon and stock. Sprinkle with salt and pepper. Stir to combine well.
2. Lock the lid. Set to Manual function and set the timer for 5 minutes at Low Pressure.
3. Once the timer goes off, press Cancel. Do a quick pressure release.
4. Carefully open the lid. Add the cream, stir, set the pot to Sauté, cook for 3 minutes more, ladle the soup into bowls and serve.

Ginger Halibut Soup

Serves: 4

Cooking Time: 12 Minutes

Ingredients:

- 1 tbsp. olive oil
- 1 large onion, chopped
- 2 cups water
- 2 tbsps. minced fresh ginger
- 1 lb. halibut, sliced
- Salt and pepper, to taste

Directions:

1. Press the Sauté button on the Instant Pot and heat the olive oil.
2. Sauté the onion for 3 minutes or until translucent.
3. Add the remaining ingredients. Stir to combine well.
4. Lock the lid. Set on the Manual mode, then set the timer to 10 minutes at Low Pressure.
5. When the timer goes off, perform a quick release.
6. Carefully open the lid. Allow to cool before serving.

Paleo Pumpkin Soup

Serves:6

Cooking Time: 15 Minutes

Ingredients:

- 2 cups almond milk
- 4 cups chicken broth
- 2 pounds raw pumpkin
- 1 tbsp cilantro, dried
- Salt and black pepper to taste
- ½ tsp cinnamon

Directions:

1. In your IP, add all the ingredients. Stir the mixture. Seal the lid, select Manual at High, and cook for 4 minutes. When ready, release the pressure naturally for 5 minutes. Serve in soup bowls.

Basic Brown Stock

Serves: 10

Cooking Time:2 Hours 10 Minutes

Ingredients:

- 2 brown onions, quartered
- 2 carrots, chopped
- 1 tablespoon olive oil
- 1 celery stalk, chopped
- 3 pounds meaty pork bones

Directions:

1. Add all ingredients to the inner pot of your Instant Pot.
2. Secure the lid. Choose the "Soup/Broth" mode and cook for 120 minutes at Low pressure. Once cooking is complete, use a natural pressure release for 10 minutes; carefully remove the lid.
3. Remove the bones and vegetables using a metal spoon with holes and discard. Pour the liquid through the sieve into the bowl.
4. Use immediately or store in your refrigerator. Bon appétit!

Sage Zucchini Soup

Serves:4

Cooking Time: 15 Minutes

Ingredients:

- 1 lb zucchini, cut into strips
- 1 tbsp dried sage
- ½ tsp garlic powder
- Salt and black pepper to taste
- 1 tsp olive oil
- 4 cups vegetable broth

Directions:

1. Place zucchini in a large bowl. Add sage, olive oil, salt, pepper, and garlic, and mix to coat thoroughly. Pour broth into the IP and add in the zucchini mixture. Seal the lid and cook for 3 minutes on Manual at High. Do a quick release and serve.

Pomodoro Soup

Serves: 8

Cooking Time: 30 Minutes

Ingredients:

- 3 tbsp vegan butter
- 1 onion, diced
- 3 lbs tomatoes, peeled and quartered
- 3½ cups vegetable broth
- 1 cup coconut cream

Directions:

1. Preheat the Instant Pot by selecting SAUTÉ. Once hot, add the butter and melt it.
2. Add the onion and sauté for 5 minutes.
3. Add the tomatoes and sauté for another 2-3 minutes.
4. Pour in the broth, stir. Close and lock the lid.
5. Press the CANCEL button to reset the cook-

ing program, then press the SOUP button and set the cooking time for 6 minutes.
6. When the timer beeps, use a Quick Release. Carefully unlock the lid.
7. Add the coconut cream and stir.
8. Select SAUTÉ again and cook for 1-2 minutes.
9. With an immersion blender, blend the soup to your desired texture. Serve.

Low Carb Chicken Noodle Soup

Serves: 2

Cooking Time: 27 Minutes

Ingredients:

- 2 tsps. coconut oil
- 1 lb. skinless and boneless chicken thighs
- 1 cup celery
- 1 cup diced carrots
- Salt, to taste
- 10½ oz. spiral daikon noodles

Directions:

1. In the Instant Pot, add the coconut oil and chicken thighs.
2. Set the Instant Pot to Sauté and cook for 10 minutes or until cooked through.
3. Shred the chicken meat with a fork and add the celery and carrots.
4. Continue cooking for 2 minutes more and season with salt.
5. Lock the lid. Change the setting to Soup and set the cooking time for 15 minutes.
6. After the timer stops, add the daikon noodles and serve.

Snacks & Desserts, Appetizers Recipes

Snacks & Desserts, Appetizers Recipes

Cinnamon Yogurt Custard

Servings: 4

Cooking Time: 1 Hour

Ingredients:

- ½ cup plain Greek yogurt
- ½ cup sweetened condensed milk
- ½ teaspoon ground cinnamon
- ¼ cup chopped fruit or berries of your choice, for garnish

Directions:

1. Place the trivet in the inner pot, then pour in 1 cup water.
2. In a heatproof bowl that fits inside the Instant Pot, mix together the yogurt, condensed milk, and cinnamon. Tightly cover the bowl with aluminum foil. Place the bowl on the trivet.
3. Lock the lid into place. Select Pressure Cook or Manual; set the pressure to High and the time to 25 minutes.
4. After the cook time is complete, let the pressure release Naturally. Unlock and remove the lid. Carefully remove the bowl. Let it cool at room temperature for 30 minutes, then refrigerate, covered, for 3 hours.
5. Serve garnished with the fruits of your choice.

Glazed Fruits

Serves: 6

Cooking Time: 12 Minutes

Ingredients:

- ½ cup honey
- ½ cup balsamic vinegar
- ¼ tsp. salt
- 6 peaches, pitted and halved
- Vanilla ice cream

Directions:

1. Set the Instant Pot on Sauté mode, add honey and balsamic vinegar, sauté for 2 minutes.
2. Add the salt and peaches, stir.
3. Lock the lid. Set the Instant Pot to Manual mode, then set the timer for 10 minutes at High Pressure.
4. When the timer goes off, perform a quick release. Carefully open the lid.
5. Divide into bowls, leave aside to cool down, add vanilla ice cream on top and serve.

Coconut Pancake

Serves: 4

Cooking Time: 40 Minutes

Ingredients:

- 1½ cups coconut milk
- 2 cups self-raising flour
- 2 eggs
- 1 tbsp. olive oil
- 2 tbsps. sugar

Directions:

1. In a bowl, mix eggs with sugar, milk and flour and whisk until you obtain a batter.
2. Grease the Instant Pot with oil, add the batter, spread into the pot.
3. Lock the lid. Set the Instant Pot to Manual mode, then set the timer for 40 minutes at Low Pressure.
4. When the timer goes off, perform a natural release for 10 minutes, then release any remaining pressure. Carefully open the lid.
5. Slice pancake, divide between plates and serve cold.

Spinach Dip

Serves:4

Cooking Time: 15 Minutes

Ingredients:

- 2 cups spinach, chopped
- 1 garlic clove, minced
- 1/3 cup coconut milk
- 1 oz cooked bacon, chopped
- 1/3 white onion, chopped

Directions:

1. Add spinach, garlic, onion, bacon, and coconut milk to the IP. Pour in ½ cup of water.

Seal the lid and press Manual. Cook at High for 4 minutes. After cooking, do a quick pressure release. Transfer to a Serves: dishes.

Crab Spread

Serves: 4

Cooking Time: 15 Minutes

Ingredients:

- 1 tsp. Worcestershire sauce
- ½ bunch scallions, chopped
- ½ cup sour cream
- ¼ cup half-and-half
- 8 oz. crab meat

Directions:

1. In the Instant Pot, mix the crabmeat with sour cream, half-and-half, scallions and Worcestershire sauce, and stir to combine well.
2. Lock the lid. Select the Manual mode, then set the timer for 15 minutes at Low Pressure.
3. Once the timer goes off, do a quick pressure release. Carefully open the lid.
4. Allow the spread cool for a few minutes and serve.

Smoked Paprika Potato Chips

Serves:4

Cooking Time: 20 Minutes

Ingredients:

- 4 russet potatoes, sliced
- ½ tsp smoked paprika
- Salt and black pepper to taste
- 2 tbsp olive oil

Directions:

1. Place the slices in the pressure cooker and pour enough water to cover them. Seal the lid, select Manual, and set the timer to 10 minutes at High. Release the pressure quickly. Drain the potatoes and discard the water. Transfer to a bowl. Wipe the cooker clean. Press Sauté, set to High, and heat the oil. Sprinkle the potatoes with paprika, salt, and pepper, and toss to combine. Be careful not to break them. When the oil is hot, add the potatoes and cook for about a minute, per side.

Poached Pears

Serves: 6

Cooking Time: 10 Minutes

Ingredients:

- 1 cup red wine
- ½ cup sugar
- 2 tsps. vanilla extract
- ¼ tsp. cinnamon
- 6 green pears

Directions:

1. In the Instant Pot, mix the wine with sugar, vanilla, cinnamon and pears.
2. Lock the lid. Set the Instant Pot to Manual mode, then set the timer for 10 minutes at High Pressure.
3. When the timer goes off, perform a quick release. Carefully open the lid.
4. Let the pears cool and transfer them to bowls. Reserve the wine sauce remains in the Instant Pot.
5. Drizzle wine sauce all over and serve.

Broccoli With Two-cheese And Chili Dip

Servings:x

Cooking Time: 15 Minutes | Servings 6

Ingredients:

- 1 cup water
- 1 ½ pounds broccoli, broken into florets
- For the Sauce:
- 1 can of chili
- 1 cup Ricotta cheese, crumbled
- 1 ¼ cups Gruyère cheese shredded
- 1/4 cup salsa

Directions:

1. Add water to the base of your Instant Pot.
2. Put the broccoli florets into the steaming basket. Transfer the steaming basket to the Instant Pot.
3. Secure the lid. Choose the "Manual" mode and High pressure; cook for 3 minutes. Once cooking is complete, use a quick pressure release; carefully remove the lid.
4. Now, cook all sauce ingredients in a sauté pan that is preheated over medium-low flame. Cook for 7 minutes or until everything is incorporated.
5. Serve steamed broccoli with the sauce on the side. Bon appétit!

Garlic Butter Shrimp

Serves: 8

Cooking Time: 10 Minutes

Ingredients:

- 1 ½ pounds shrimp, deveined
- 1/2 stick butter
- 1/4 cup soy sauce
- 2 garlic cloves, minced
- Sea salt and ground black pepper, to taste
- 2 tablespoons fresh scallions, chopped

Directions:

1. Throw all ingredients, except for the scallions, into the inner pot of your Instant Pot.
2. Secure the lid. Choose the "Manual" mode and cook for 4 minutes at High pressure. Once cooking is complete, use a quick pressure release; carefully remove the lid.
3. Transfer your shrimp to a nice serving bowl. The sauce will thicken as it cools. Garnish with fresh scallions and serve with toothpicks.

Coconut And Avocado Pudding

Serves: 3

Cooking Time: 2 Minutes

Ingredients:

- 14 oz. canned coconut milk
- 1 tbsp. cocoa powder
- 1 avocado, pitted, peeled and chopped
- 4 tbsps. sugar
- ½ cup avocado oil

Directions:

1. In a bowl, mix oil with cocoa powder and half of the sugar, stir well, transfer to a lined container, keep in the fridge for 1 hour and chop into small pieces.
2. In the Instant Pot, mix coconut milk with avocado and the rest of the sugar, blend using an immersion blender.
3. Lock the lid. Set the Instant Pot to Manual mode, then set the timer for 2 minutes at High Pressure.
4. When the timer goes off, perform a natural release. Carefully open the lid.
5. Add chocolate chips, stir, divide pudding into bowls and keep in the fridge until you serve it.

Awesome Nutella Cakes

Servings: 6

Cooking Time: 35 Minutes

Ingredients:

- 1 cup Nutella
- 2 large eggs
- ¼ cup plain flour
- 14 blueberries + for serving

Directions:

1. In a medium bowl, whisk Nutella and eggs until smoothly combined. Add flour and mix well. Grease 6 holes of a silicone egg bite tray with cooking spray and fill halfway with Nutella mixture. Drop two blueberries into each hole and cover with the remaining Nutella mixture.
2. Wrap muffin tray with foil. Pour 1 cup of water into your Instant Pot, fit in a trivet, and place egg bite tray on top. Seal the lid, select Manual/Pressure Cook on High, and set to 18 minutes. After cooking, do a quick pressure release, and unlock the lid. Carefully remove the tray, take off the foil, allow cooling for 10 minutes, and pop out dessert bites. Serve immediately or chill for later use.

Honey-glazed Baby Carrots

Servings:x

Cooking Time: 15 Minutes | Servings 6

Ingredients:

- 1 ½ cups water
- 2 ½ pounds baby carrots, trimmed
- 1 teaspoon thyme
- 1 teaspoon dill
- Salt and white pepper, to taste
- 2 tablespoons coconut oil
- 1/4 cup honey

Directions:

1. Add 1 ½ cups of water to the base of your Instant Pot.
2. Now, arrange baby carrots in the steaming basket. Transfer the steaming basket to the Instant Pot.
3. Secure the lid and choose the "Manual" function; cook for 3 minutes at High pressure. Once cooking is complete, use a quick release; carefully remove the lid.
4. Strain baby carrots and reserve.
5. Then, add the other ingredients to the Instant Pot. Press the "Sauté" button and cook until everything is heated through.
6. Add reserved baby carrots and gently stir. Bon appétit!

Grandma's Pear And Peach Compote

Serves:4

Cooking Time: 2hours And 15 Minutes

Ingredients:

- 2 ½ cups peaches, chopped
- 2 cups pears, diced
- Juice of 1 orange
- 2 tbsp cornstarch
- ¼ tsp cinnamon

Directions:

1. Place the peaches, pears, ½ cup of water, and orange juice, in the IP. Stir to combine and seal the lid, select Manual, and set to 3 minutes at High. Do a quick pressure release. Press Sauté and whisk in the cornstarch and cinnamon. Cook until the compote thickens, for 5 minutes. When thickened, transfer to an airtight container and refrigerate for at least 2 hours.

Chili Endives Platter

Serves: 4

Cooking Time: 7 Minutes

Ingredients:

- ¼ tsp. chili powder
- 1 tbsp. butter
- 4 trimmed and halved endives
- 1 tbsp. lemon juice
- Salt, to taste

Directions:

1. Set the Instant Pot to Sauté and melt the butter. Add the endives, salt, chili powder and lemon juice to the pot.
2. Lock the lid. Select the Manual mode, then set the timer for 7 minutes at High Pressure.
3. Once the timer goes off, do a quick pressure release. Carefully open the lid.
4. Divide the endives into bowls. Drizzle some cooking juice over them and serve.

Caramel Corns

Servings: 4

Cooking Time: 15 Minutes

Ingredients:

- 4 tbsp butter
- 1 cup sweet corn kernels
- 3 tbsp brown sugar
- ¼ cup whole milk

Directions:

1. Set your Instant Pot to Sauté, melt butter, and mix in corn kernels. Once heated and popping, cover the top with a clear instant pot safe lid, and continue cooking until corn stops popping for 3 minutes.
2. Open the lid and transfer popcorns to a bowl. Press Cancel and wipe the inner pot clean. Select Sauté. Combine in brown sugar and milk and cook with frequent stirring until sugar dissolves and sauce coats the back of the spoon, 3-4 minutes. Turn Instant Pot off. Drizzle caramel sauce all over corns and toss to coat thoroughly. Cool and serve.

Maple-glazed Carrots

Servings:4

Cooking Time: 20 Minutes

Ingredients:

- 1 pound baby carrots
- 1½ tablespoons unsalted butter
- 1½ tablespoons pure maple syrup
- ¼ teaspoon kosher salt
- Pinch freshly ground black pepper
- 1 teaspoon minced fresh thyme

Directions:

1. Combine the carrots and 1 cup water in the inner pot.
2. Lock the lid into place. Select Pressure Cook or Manual; set the pressure to High and the time to 2 minutes.
3. After the cook time is complete, Quick release the pressure. Unlock and remove the lid. Drain the carrots in a colander and return them to the pot.
4. Select Sauté, set the heat to Medium, and add the butter, maple syrup, salt, and pepper. Cook, stirring, for 2 to 3 minutes, until the carrots are coated in the sauce. Sprinkle with the thyme. Serve hot or warm.

Poached Eggs With Watercress

Serves: 1

Cooking Time: 10 Minutes

Ingredients:

- 2 eggs
- 1 cup watercress, chopped
- ½ cup water
- ¼ tsp garlic powder
- Salt and black pepper to taste

Directions:

1. In a bowl, whisk eggs and water. Add the remaining ingredients and stir well. Transfer the mixture to a heat-proof bowl, that fits in your instant pot.
2. Add 1 cup of water in the pot. Set the steamer tray and place the bowl on top. Seal the lid and cook on High Pressure for 5 minutes. Do a quick release.

Chicken Dip

Serves: 6

Cooking Time: 15 Minutes

Ingredients:

- 1 cup Greek yogurt
- 4 oz. cream cheese
- ½ cup hot sauce
- 3 cups cooked and shredded chicken
- 1 cup shredded Mozzarella cheese

Directions:

1. In the Instant Pot, mix chicken with cream cheese and hot sauce, and stir to combine well.
2. Lock the lid. Select the Manual mode, then set the timer for 15 minutes at High Pressure.
3. Once the timer goes off, do a natural pressure release for 10 minutes, then release any remaining pressure. Carefully open the lid.
4. Add the yogurt and Mozzarella cheese. Give the mixture a good stir. Let rest for about 8 minutes, then serve.

Chocolate-strawberry Bars

Serves:6

Cooking Time: 20 Minutes

Ingredients:

- ½ cup almond butter
- 2 cups strawberries
- 2 tbsp cocoa powder

Directions:

1. Place strawberries and almond butter in a bowl and mash with a fork. Add in cocoa powder and stir until well combined. Pour the strawberry and almond butter in a greased baking dish. Pour 1 cup of water in the pressure cooker and lower a trivet. Place the baking dish on top of the trivet and seal the lid. Select Manual and cook for 15 minutes at High. When it goes off, do a quick release. Let cool before cutting into squares.

Chocolate Fondue

Serves: 3-6

Cooking Time: 25 Minutes

Ingredients:

- One 100 g bar dark chocolate 70-85%, cut into large chunks
- 1 tbsp sugar
- 1 tsp amaretto liqueur
- ½ cup heavy cream
- 2 cups water

Directions:

1. Divide the chocolate, sugar, amaretto liqueur, and heavy cream between 3 ramekins.
2. Pour the water into the Instant Pot and set a steam rack in the pot.
3. Place the ramekins on the rack. Close and lock the lid.
4. Select MANUAL and cook at HIGH pressure for 3 minutes.
5. When cooking is complete, let the pressure Release Naturally for 10 minutes. Release any remaining steam manually. Uncover the pot.
6. Remove the ramekins from the pot.
7. Using a fork quickly stir the contents of the ramekins vigorously for about 1 minute, until the texture is smooth and thick.
8. Serve with fresh fruit or bread pieces.

Conclusion

In conclusion, the Instant Pot represents a significant advancement in kitchen technology, fundamentally changing how we approach cooking. Its multifaceted design combines the functions of multiple appliances into one sleek and efficient device, providing users with the ability to prepare a wide range of dishes quickly and with minimal effort. The time-saving capabilities of the Instant Pot are particularly beneficial in today's fast-paced world, allowing families and individuals to enjoy homemade meals without spending hours in the kitchen.

Moreover, the nutritional advantages of pressure cooking cannot be overlooked. By cooking foods quickly and retaining their natural flavors and nutrients, the Instant Pot empowers health-conscious individuals to create wholesome meals that are both satisfying and beneficial to their well-being. This advantage appeals to a growing number of consumers who prioritize healthy eating but may not have the time or knowledge to cook elaborate meals from scratch.

The user-friendly design of the Instant Pot, coupled with its intuitive interface and pre-set cooking programs, makes it accessible for cooks of all skill levels. Whether you are a seasoned chef or a novice in the kitchen, the Instant Pot provides a simple yet powerful way to explore new recipes, experiment with flavors, and achieve consistent results. Its versatility allows users to adapt it to various dietary preferences and cooking styles, further enhancing its appeal.

As we continue to embrace the convenience of modern appliances, the Instant Pot stands out as a symbol of innovation in home cooking. It encourages creativity in the kitchen and fosters a love for cooking by making it more approachable and less intimidating. By investing in an Instant Pot, you are not just acquiring a kitchen gadget; you are embracing a lifestyle that prioritizes health, efficiency, and culinary exploration.

In summary, the Instant Pot is more than just a cooking appliance; it is a game-changer for home cooks everywhere. By combining speed, convenience, and nutritional benefits, it has earned its place as an essential tool for modern kitchens, making healthy, delicious meals attainable for everyone. Whether you're cooking for a family, entertaining guests, or simply preparing a meal for yourself, the Instant Pot can elevate your culinary experience and inspire a newfound appreciation for the art of cooking.

MEASUREMENT CONVERSIONS

BASIC KITCHEN CONVERSIONS & EQUIVALENT

DRY MEASUREMENTS CONVERSION CHART
3 TEASPOONS = 1 TABLESPOON = 1/16 CUP
6 TEASPOONS = 2 TABLESPOONS = 1/8 CUP
12 TEASPOONS = 4 TABLESPOONS = 1/4 CUP
24 TEASPOONS = 8 TABLESPOONS = 1/2 CUP
36 TEASPOONS = 12 TABLESPOONS = 3/4 CUP
48 TEASPOONS = 16 TABLESPOONS = 1 CUP

METRIC TO US COOKING CONVER SIONS

OVEN TEMPERATURE
120℃ = 250° F
160℃ = 320° F
180℃ = 350° F
205℃ = 400° F
220℃ = 425° F

OVEN TEMPERATURE
8 FLUID OUNCES = 1 CUP = 1/2 PINT = 1/4 QUART
16 FLUID OUNCES = 2 CUPS = 1 PINT = 1/2 QUART
32 FLUID OUNCES = 4 CUPS = 2 PINTS = 1 QUART= 1/4 GALLON
128 FLUID OUNCES = 16 CUPS = 8 PINTS = 4 QUARTS = 1 GALLON

BAKING IN GRAMS
1 CUP FLOUR = 140 GRAMS
1 CUP SUGAR = 150 GRAMS
1 CUP POWDERED SUGAR = 160 GRAMS
1 CUP HEAVY CREAM = 235 GRAMS

VOLUME
1 CUP FLOUR = 140 GRAMS
1 CUP SUGAR = 150 GRAMS
1 CUP POWDERED SUGAR = 160 GRAMS
1 CUP HEAVY CREAM = 235 GRAMS

WEIGHT

1 GRAM = .035 OUNCES
100 GRAMS = 3.5 OUNCES
500 GRAMS = 1.1 POUNDS
1 KILOGRAM = 35 OUNCES

BUTTER

1 CUP BUTTER = 2 STICKS = 8 OUNCES = 230 GRAMS = 8 TABLESPOONS

BUTTER

1 CUP = 8 FLUID OUNCES
1 CUP = 16 TABLESPOONS
1 CUP = 48 TEASPOONS
1 CUP = 1/2 PINT
1 CUP = 1/4 QUART
1 CUP = 1/16 GALLON
1 CUP = 240 ML

BAKING PAN CONVERSIONS

9-INCH ROUND CAKE PAN = 12 CUPS
10-INCH TUBE PAN =16 CUPS
11-INCH BUNDT PAN = 12 CUPS
9-INCH SPRINGFORM PAN = 10 CUPS
9 X 5 INCH LOAF PAN = 8 CUPS
9-INCH SQUARE PAN = 8 CUPS

US TO METRIC COOKING CONVERSIONS

1/5 TSP = 1 ML
1 TSP = 5 ML
1 TBSP = 15 ML
1 FL OUNCE = 30 ML
1 CUP = 237 ML
1 PINT (2 CUPS) = 473 ML
1 QUART (4 CUPS) = .95 LITER
1 GALLON (16 CUPS) = 3.8 LITERS
1 OZ = 28 GRAMS
1 POUND = 454 GRAMS

US TO METRIC COOKING CONVERSIONS

1/5 TSP = 1 ML
1 TSP = 5 ML
1 TBSP = 15 ML
1 FL OUNCE = 30 ML
1 CUP = 237 ML
1 PINT (2 CUPS) = 473 ML
1 QUART (4 CUPS) = .95 LITER
1 GALLON (16 CUPS) = 3.8 LITERS
1 OZ = 28 GRAMS
1 POUND = 454 GRAMS

HEALTE RECORD TRACKER

_____   _____

_____   _____

_____   _____

_____   _____

_____   _____

_____   _____

_____   _____

_____   _____

_____   _____

How to Reduce Food Waste

Plan Meals: Create a weekly meal plan and shopping list.

Store Food Properly: Use airtight containers and maintain the right temperature.

FIFO Rule: Consume older items before newer ones.

Portion Control: Serve smaller portions to avoid leftovers.

Use Leftovers: Repurpose or freeze them.

Understand Expiry Dates: Many foods are safe past these dates.

Composting: Start a compost bin for food scraps.

Donate: Share surplus non-perishables with food banks.

Shop Mindfully: Buy in bulk, choose minimal packaging.

Batch Cooking: Prep and freeze meals for later.

Preserve Foods: Learn canning, pickling, and drying.

Spread Awareness: Educate and inspire others.

Recipe for:

Ingredients:

Equipment:

Description:

Instructions:

Recipe ....

From the kicthen of ....

Serves .... Prep time .... Cook time ....

☐ Difficulty   ☐ Easy   ☐ Medium   ☐ Hard

Ingredient

....

....

....

....

....

Directions ....

....

....

....

....

....

....

Recipe ....

From the kicthen of ....

Serves .... Prep time .... Cook time ....

☐ Difficulty ☐ Easy ☐ Medium ☐ Hard

Ingredient

Yummy!

....

....

....

....

....

Directions ....

....

....

....

....

....

....

....

RECITES

DATE

RECIPES		Salads	Meats	Soups
SERVES		Grains	Seafood	Snack
PREP TIME		Breads	Vegetables	Breakfast
COOK TIME		Appetizers	Desserts	Lunch
FROM THE KITCHEN OF		Main Dishes	Beverages	Dinners

INGREDIENTS

DIRECTIONS

NOTES

SERVING	☆☆☆☆☆
DIFFICULTY	☆☆☆☆☆
OVERALL	☆☆☆☆☆

APPENDIX : RECIPES INDEX

Made in the USA
Columbia, SC
02 January 2025

51007643R00057